THE EVANGELICAL
RESPONSE TO BANGKOK

EDITED BY
DR. RALPH WINTER

William Carey Library

SOUTH PASADENA, CALIF. 91030

Library of Congress Catalog Card Number 73-80166
International Standard Book Number 0-87808-125-9

Published by the William Carey Library

PRINTED IN THE UNITED STATES OF AMERICA

Contents

Preface

In this permissive age we can save money by cutting
our hair at home, and we can reduce book prices by
short-circuiting costly typesetting. In the case of
this book you can easily tell which chapters were written from scratch for this book, since they are the typewritten sections. One exception is McGavran's which
is retyped from *The Church Growth Bulletin,* which is
itself typewritten. The other exception is the chapter
by Paul Rees, which he very kindly turned over in type-
set format. We are indebted to the original publishers
of all the other materials for lending, in effect, their
investment in the typesetting of their material.

The multi-format appearance of this book bespeaks the
unpretensious spirit with which it is offered. It is
not, in sum, an attack. It simply brings together some
of the evangelical conversation about Bangkok. The purpose is to foster understanding, not forestall it. In
this sense it is as much intended for those who do not
normally call themselves evangelicals as for those who
do.

It is an unfinished story. The responses themselves
are honest, if preliminary. They may leave one unsatis-
fied. The real response, the response that is most critical, is the response we all make in these days to our
living Lord. To facilitate that end this modest collection, made in haste, in sincerely offered.

Acknowledgements

We wish to express appreciation to the editors of the following periodicals for permission to reprint:

The *Evangelical Missions Quarterly* for the chapters entitled "A Look at Bangkok in Historical Perspective" by Jack Shepherd, "Disneyland at Bangkok" by C. Peter Wagner, and "Salvation--Yesterday, Tomorrow and Today" by Arthur Glasser, all of which appeared in Vol. 9, No. 3 (Spring, 1973) of that periodical.

The Church Growth Bulletin (Vol. IX, No. 1, Sept., 1972) for "Salvation Today" by Donald A. McGavran.

The *International Review of Mission* (Vol. LXI, No. 243, July, 1972) for "Conceptual Dyads in the Ethnotheology of 'Salvation Today' by A.R. Tippett.

Eternity (April, 1973) for "What Evangelicals Can Learn from Bangkok" by William J. Petersen and Dr. Arthur Glasser.

World Vision (March, 1973) for "Two Evangelicals Look at the Bangkok Consultation" by C. Peter Wagner and Arthur F. Glasser.

Christianity Today (Vol. XVII, No. 13, March 30, 1973) for "The Theology of Salvation at Bangkok" by Peter Beyerhaus and "Dateline: Bangkok" by Harold Lindsell. Also to the same magazine for the Feb. 2, 1973 appearance of Donald Hoke's article entitled "Salvation Isn't the Same Today."

Introduction:

WHY AN EVANGELICAL RESPONSE TO BANGKOK?

Ralph D. Winter

I was not there. While I acted as a Spanish-to-English translator at the first meeting of the CWME in Mexico City in 1963, I obviously have only a vague feeling for what it was like at Bangkok, ten years later, where there was a considerably larger third-world representation. But in any case it is not my task in this introduction to add or subtract from the responses constituting the chapters of this book. Rather, it falls on my shoulders as the editor to explain why I feel this book "had to be".

For one thing, the title must not be interpreted as THE Evangelical Response to Bangkok. I have not pulled together any kind of definitive, much less authorized or authoritative point of view on behalf of the evangelical movement. Not only are many additional "responses" left out that are equally evangelical: the wide range of responses included in this little volume are not really *a* single response, much less *the* response. In fact, some will say, after perusing these pages, that evangelicals obviously present no clearcut position. The very variety of opinions, then, is proof that the title does not read properly if the word *THE* is emphasized.

Rather, the second word, EVANGELICAL, is the one that requires emphasis. The whole world was watching Bangkok. There have been many responses from many

1

quarters. Here we are simply trying to give the reader
some feel for the *evangelical* response to Bangkok.

WHO ARE THE EVANGELICALS?

In so saying, of course, we are pushed back to a
still prior question: "Who do you mean by *the evangelicals*?" Since a key purpose of this book is to
allow these responses to tell us more about evangelicals (as well as more about Bangkok), it will be a
major task in this introduction to make clear what
we mean by the term *evangelical*, so that the book can
help the evangelicals whoever they are, be better un-
derstood--by themselves and by others.

Curiously, a study of the evangelical response
to Bangkok happens to provide highly significant in-
sight into the nature of the evangelical movement.
Why? Because no Christian movement in the Protestant
tradition has been more consistently associated with
what has long been called "foreign missions" than the
evangelical movement--at least with what I am here
calling the *evangelical movement*.

Probably no brand-new observer on the scene at
Bangkok would have ever guessed it, but I believe it
is possible to say that no meeting associated with,
or in any way sponsored by the WCC has ever been as
extensively the direct result of the force of the
evangelical movement as the meeting at Bangkok. This
will be detailed later. Ironically, however, self-
conscious evangelicals at Bangkok were at the very
fringe, at best, or only in the corridors as visitors
or press men, at worst. To many readers it may simply be unbelievable that I should claim Bangkok was in
any sense the *result* of the evangelical movement.
This assertion, unsupported at this point, may at
least give some clue as to the historical dimension
of a great deal of what I will say.

Are Evangelicals Conservative?

Let me anticipate one specific reaction: why
don't I utilize the phrase *conservative evangelical*?

Don't I know that the people who go around calling
themselves *evangelicals* are more and more identified
as a movement and are called *conservative evangelicals*,
at least by those who don't usually characterize themselves as evangelicals? Am I bridling at the accepted
label? Yes.

I don't want to make a big point out of this. I
really only introduce it to clarify things, and because it leads to one of the key elements in the picture. I recognize that many Christian groups end up
accepting the labels dreamed up for them by outsiders
--so *Methodists, Quakers, Presbyterians, Franciscans,
Jesuits,* and even the early *Christians.* After all,
you've got to be able to talk, and you might as well
employ symbolic referents that are well-established.
I recognize furthermore that many evangelicals are
acquiescing to the label *conservative evangelicals.*
I do myself when there is no time to explain.

However, as I say, I resist this label if only to
make a point. The point is that most evangelicals
still do not employ the imposed label, that only in
historical theological tomes nowadays is the word *evangelical* used to refer to a now-ancient Protestant tradition, and, anyway, even Martin Marty, who is always
up to date, consents to the single word, *evangelical,*
(and this is not because he ordinarily counts himself
among those who call themselves simply *evangelical.*)
I may add that in my own church (United Presbyterian,
USA) well-intentioned unifiers insist that (in the
historic sense) all our people are *evangelicals,* but
in my opinion this practice only obscures and confuses
differences that need to be better understood, not
wished away.

As a matter of fact, most participants in the
modern evangelical movement cannot quite understand
what the fuss is all about. They are quite ignorant
of the fact that there ever was an Evangelical Synod
back in the Germany of early Protestant history. If
they knew, and if they knew much about it, they would
probably consider it non-evangelical! More surprising,
most evangelicals really don't know much about that
other immense reformation called (often) the *Evangelical*

Awakening. This of course means modern evangelicals
don't even know why they call themselves evangelicals
(since the Evangelical Awakening really is the source
of *their* meaning of the word.) Least of all would
the average person-who-calls-himself-evangelical
(hereafter just *evangelical*, OK?) be prepared to discover that for over a thousand years the "evangelicals"
were those dedicated monastics and Friars who strove
to follow quite literally "the evangelical counsels"
of the four gospels.

Back to the present day: It looks right now that
the latter part of the 70s are going to be pretty much
an evangelical show. This may not be proper for an
evangelical to say. I should rather quote, apprecia-
tively, what the media people are saying. But I don't
have the time to do that. We all read the media.
Marty I can cite (*Context*, December 15, 1972). He
lavs it on the line in a very neat analysis. He takes
a whole issue to do this, precisely because the evangelical movement is simply growing and growing while
old-line churches are shrinking. My church, in last
week's General Assembly, heard that its membership
had declined to what it was 18 years ago. And you
may be sure that the local churches in my denomination that *did* grow (whose growth thus conceals the
full scope of decline in other local churches) were
very likely, with some notable exceptions, the evangelical brand. But this statement could be irritating
as well as unilluminating and unhelpful if we do not
go on to define more effectively just what it is that
allows one local church, or lone Christian, to be
called evangelical and another not.

The adjective *conservative*, in any case is not
very helpful in describing today's evangelical. Kelly's
interesting book, *Why Conservative Churches are Growing*, for example, is mis-titled. It is really a book
that tries to describe why old-line churches are dy-
ing. It does not even attempt to prove that all conservative churches are growing, since they surely are
not. He does suggest that any solid growth likely
leans on well-defined, well-understood convictions.
But *conservative* convictions? The word does not even
have a clear meaning. The fact that Kelly's conservative

churches are not just evangelical churches shows how
little affinity there really is between *conservative*
and *evangelical*.

Furthermore, *conservative* does not effectively
describe the Evangelical Awakening, nor the now world-
wide extension of that massive, renewing impulse in
the 1700s. Modern evangelicals, stung by complaints
that they have no social message, have dredged up historical evidence to the effect that their early prophets (from Wesley to William Booth) were radical
social reformers as well as evangelists. What they
don't understand is that for the most of evangelical
history the greatest religious and theological opponents of the evangelicals can only be described as
theological conservatives, who fought the innovations
and "new measures" every step of the way. The hymns
of Isaac Watts and Charles Wesley had to wait in line
more than 100 years even to gain begrudged space in
hymnals controlled by religious conservatives, the
same "morphological" conservatives who still feel that
the best liturgy is whatever Calvin and Luther cannon-
ized. The conservatives have opposed the evangelicals!

Conservative? Evangelicals have, partly due to
their non-rational mystic element, been if anything
predisposed to changes in form. The whole history of
American Protestantism, from the earliest stirrings of
evangelicalism (Theodore Freylinghusen, Jonathan Ed-
wards, Gilbert Tennant, etc.) to Billy Graham and Oral
Roberts of today, the whole history, I say, has been
one vast series of creative deviations from accepted
norms.

But it will be said, aren't most evangelicals
conservative about something? How about the Virgin
Birth--don't they all adhere to that? First of all,
anthropologists will tell you that every social group
is conservative about something, and that you can find
both truly liberal spirits and truly narrow spirits in
both "liberal" and "conservative" groups. In each case
the qualities are measured in relation to a particular,
often highly arbitrary continuum of whatever for that
group is acceptable/unacceptable. But secondly, it is

a simple historical fact that in America the evangelical movement has been responsible for at least its
share of avant-garde, even heretical splinters. However, the main thing is simply the limited usefulness
of any kind of negative or narrow theological description of evangelicals. Kentucky Fried Chicken comprehensively characterizes Kentucky about as well as the
doctrine of the Virgin Birth characterizes evangelicals.

Is There an Evangelical Essence?

All right, you say, if *conservative* does not effectively describe the evangelical, then what does?
It is much more useful in explaining the chief concern
evangelicals have about Bangkok if we ask what they are
for not just what they are *against*.

The early evangelicals preached a gospel of liberating bondage. They sought to harness men's hearts to
the will of the living God, so that their lives could
be liberated in worship and service. Compared to much
evangelical preaching today, it was an effort "to bring
about obedience to the faith," far more than seeking
mere intellectual consent. The result was expected to
be practical holiness coupled with a new kind of as-
surance in the everyday life of the believer. This
potent combination characterized by the famous phrase
"the expulsive power of a new affection" discloses the
engine behind this almost-new brand of Christianity.
It involved unprecedentedly greater emphasis upon the
observable "fruits of the Holy Spirit" in-wrought in
the personality of the believer. In the small, now-
virtually extinct "class meeting" of the Wesleyan
movement something remotely akin to sensitivity training or small group dynamics went on and the necessary,
anticipated (sometimes faked) revolution in personality gave a profound stamp of identity to the new
movement.

This English and American outworking of continental
pietism encountered in England, and especially in the
American colonies, a much less oppressive social context. Despite all Wesley's opponents and government-
backed ecclesiastical obstacles, the atmosphere he and

his hundreds of lay preachers faced was relatively
free compared to the continental scene. But in America, depending on the colony, there was generally even
greater actual freedom; after the Revolution all political restraints vanished. The net result: strong,
new, organized movements appeared that exist today.
The Presbyterian Synod of New Jersey was first split,
greatly strengthened and then united. The Methodist
church appeared out of nowhere. The Baptists in the
U.S., with air to breathe, and new evangelical winds
in their sails, encompassed the new land and went to
the ends of the earth. One Baptist left the oppressive atmosphere of England for India and now there
are twice as many Baptists in India as in England.
Why, there are more Baptists in Burma than in all
non-Russian Europe. Even the Lutherans in the U.S.
imbibed a new ingredient that disturbs them to this
day.

But as more Presbyterians and Lutherans arrived
from the old country, the evangelical element in the
U.S. faced new challenges and an older-Protestant
counter-balancing. Churches with European counterparts may have gone evangelical by the 1830s, but the
made-in-USA churches such as the Seventh-Day Adven-
tists, and the Methodists (whose European counterparts
were themselves evangelical) were able to retain their
distinctive evangelical traits much longer, despite
the onslaught of massive non-evangelical immigration.
But it would in any case be a great mistake to suppose that the evangelical movement, properly understood, could be or should be simply an ecclesiastical
phenomenon. It was rather a new spirit, a new set of
expectations about what a true Christian was really
like.

In some cases this new spirit actually split
churches: as mentioned, the Presbyterians, during
the Great Awakening in the Middle Colonies. But even
the Mennonite colonies in Russia parted ways as a result of the invasion of this new influence, producing
a new group, the Mennonite Brethren, whose characteristic evangelical traits are clearly evident to this
day.

But no church, as such, can properly be called evangelical if we intend by the word to refer to a new set of expectations resulting from heart-commitment. The reason is that churches are generally biologically perpetuating, while evangelical Christianity (some would say *true* Christianity) by its very nature cannot be. There are churches that call themselves *evangelical*, but apparently none for whom the label does not become an empty misnomer after five generations. A new set of expectations cannot be biologically transmitted, nor even culturally transmitted, if they involve the necessity of a spiritual choice, a commitment that goes beyond any kind of remorseless social influence. This fact is the rock upon which perfectionistic, utopian, or idealistic groups have been shipwrecked.

No, the evangelical movement must remain merely a movement in our description or we lose sight of its most significant characteristic, its emphasis upon the quite literal spiritual transformation of the individual. Just as "all Israel is not Israel," (e.g. the community of faith was not in every individual's case a faithful community,) so the evangelical movement carries with it, especially today, a great number of watered-down, broken-down, cooled-down, yea frozen-over and even icy-hearted "evangelicals" who, while they adhere nominally to the movement are alien to its true spirit. But so long as the movement itself is not entirely institutional, like a church, the locus of the movement can gradually, invisibly shift away from any given church, whether or not it is labelled evangelical.

Perhaps the greatest single mutation in the evangelical movement has been the recent emergence of the Pentecostal wing. This phenomenon is represented by the author (Gaxiola) of one of our chapters, is either parallel to (yet one step beyond) the evangelical movement, or it is simply the most significant neo-evangelical force today. That is, all Pentecostals tend to consider themselves evangelical but not vice versa. However, there is a great deal of affinity between these two confluent, expanding streams, and, just as

with earlier evangelicals, some Pentecostals have gone
out and started whole new denominations that are explicitly Pentecostal while others remain as "parties"
within the older churches, where, depending on their
reception, they may be a cooperative element or an
irritation. Again, as with older evangelicalism,
Pentecostalism today cannot be defined by a list of
churches--it is a movement that cuts across (in its
so-called "charismatic" form) almost all other churches;
it is so decentralized in its still early vigor that
no one school, hero, book, organization or mecca provides it complete unity, although the Full Gospel Busi-
nessmen's Fellowship International comes close to
doing so.

WHAT HAVE EVANGELICALS TO DO WITH BANGKOK?

Let's note well this powerful, fast-moving international non-ecclesiastical organization (the FGBMFI),
which has its own weekly TV show, a magazine with half-
a-million circulation, and grand-ballroom-packed meetings in major hotels, as well as vigorous chapters all
over the U. S. and around the world. It is simply one
more parallel on the part of Pentecostalism to a major
characteristic of the main stream of the older evangelical movement: evangelicalism employs a vast jungle
of para-church structures the very existence of which
the average non-evangelical protestant (and the average
participant at Bangkok) does not have even the remotest,
faintest idea. This is not a recent phenomenon. The
vast, fascinating "Evangelical Empire" so fiercely resented by certain church leaders in the 1830s was the
first dramatic evidence of this evangelical tendency to
downplay ethnic and cultural elements in the religious
distinctives of the older church traditions and to co-
operate in a multitude of para-church service agencies.
(In the process huge amounts of theology are also li-
berally ignored, save for a visible core, which then
somehow signals "conservatism.")

Are Evangelicals Structurally and Psychologically
Out-of-Phase?

Both then and now this degree of cooperation
could have been hailed as the most ecumenical phenomenon ever. However, this kind of non- or para-
ecclesiastical cooperation doesn't count in ecclesiastical circles. It is more likely resented. Yet
it is precisely this flourishing of "new movements"
which Latourette stressed as the truest evidence of
vitality!

However, the relative invisibility of the evangelical empire of today is by no means due merely to
ecclesiastical reticence. It is partly due to the
fact that churches are by nature more visible: being
mostly democratic in structure, their members, can
and do demand by orderly process, to know where the
money is going. Except for the likelihood of a certain tiny amount of a Watergate-type of concealed di-
version of funds, the program agencies of the major
churches have a whole lot better track record of self-
exposure than do most of the para-ecclesiastical structures, which ordinarily are not subject to the same
disclosure requirements. This lack of built-in accountability in the para-organizations is one of the
concerns for which the United Presbyterian Center for
Mission Studies (Box 2613, Fullerton, Calif. 92633) was
established, itself a carefully accountable *intra*-
denominational para-ecclesiastical structure dedicated
to the evaluation of all para-ecclesiastical structures
involved in cross-cultural mission.

For these para structures there is another kind
of very important built-in accountability that operates
in the long-run as a chastening and refining agent:
the simple fact that donors, evangelical donors, must
be pleased. Elements in the vast evangelical empire
of para-church structures may now and then bamboozle
people for a while, but the inter-locking nature of the
leadership of all true *movements* has the ultimate pre-
requisite of informal internal communication that can
bring all kinds of pressures to bear. Billy Graham's
widely-quoted approval of the *Living Bible*, for example,

shows the symbiosis between two evangelical para-church
structures that otherwise have no organizational connection. That is, the presence or absence of this
kind of resonance can make a great deal of difference
in the confidence of potential donors, and thus to the
life of the structure.

This kind of "pocket veto" power functions within
church-sponsored programs too, but only as a tragic
emergency procedure where a suddenly discovered great
distance between donor and decisions, an anti-insti-
tutional mood, or flagrant mis-steps, sweep confidence
away from the regular procedures of orderly representation of voting power, regular procedures totally absent in the case of most para-structures. The sudden
discovery of great distance is an inherent problem:
the local pew-dwellers find the local church easier to
monitor than the national church let alone the National
Council or World Council of Churches. In my church the
phenomenon of unbroken increase of *local* funds through
a period of a 25% fall-off of funds at the *national*
level seems to give conflicting signals, but it really
doesn't. People nowadays are not less interested but
more interested, more inquiring, more eager than ever
to participate, and the massive decentralization ir-
resistably taking place may herald the wrong things
if it is not properly interpreted. I hesitantly suggest that all of this is in part a creeping *evangelical*
tendency away from ecclesiocentric service initiative.

Why are Evangelicals congenitally suspicious of
churches in general and Bangkok in particular? Because the evangelical movement, as with Pietism before
it, was born in a cold crib of entrenched clerical
hostility. Because evangelicals have found only the
para-church structure to be continuously available to
their initiative. Because the evangelical movement
gained birth and struggled into life during a period
of unprecedentedly successful secular revulsion against
political tyranny. No one not born in the U. S. can
easily sense the instinctive, deep-stamped, peculiarly
"American" ultra-sensitivity to control from the top.
It is a veritable mania among many. While the mute
peasants who stayed in the old country may have had

far greater cause to voice their resentment of all
pyramidal power structures, the "American Experience"
was one which in both secular and religious spheres
allowed the free expression of all those suppressed
sentiments and thus produced a mind-set which in its
religious expression has been practically a recipe for
fission and fragmentation in *church* structures, but
wide task-oriented cooperation in *para-church* structures.

Thus the evangelical response to Bangkok carries
with it a great deal of individualistic Americanism,
not just evangelical piety. The very impossibility
of disentangling this element in dialogue with the
American evangelical is overwhelming. The eventual
"Americanization" of the Roman tradition is one of
the most extensive, titanic organizational transmu-
tations in history. Scepticism of government, reaction
to authority, sensitivity to the loss of grass-roots
control, all this is the air American evengelicals
breathe. Don't knock it altogether! This is a major
ingredient in the anti-colonial nationalism spawned
by (evangelical) mission schools around the world!

Do Evangelicals Have a Proprietary Interest in Bangkok?

There is a final, inherent element in the evangelicals' response to the WCC and specifically to
Bangkok, to which we have only briefly alluded. This
is most delicate. How could these miserable, suspicious, anti-conciliar evangelicals have any right what-
soever to be heard on Bangkok? Why don't these anti-
council, anti-COCU spoilers just stay away, stay away
from Bangkok and stay away from the subject?

It is the greatest of ironies that Bangkok, the
CWME itself (even more than the WCC), is quite specifically the offspring—not even a stepchild—of the
evangelical mission empire. We have not said much thus
far about the foreign mission movement in the Protestant tradition and the fact that this truly amazing
worldwide enterprise (even less understood, if not less
prominent, than the para-church empire in general) is
98 and 44/100ths percent evangelical in its overall

history. Apart from this enterprise there never would
have been the basis, either in "the mission lands"
or in the "home lands" for the development of the
International Missionary Council. I have no desire to
"rub this in". But it is, clearly, the basis for considerable evangelical "proprietary" interest in what
went on at Bangkok. Bangkok would inevitably "betray"
this interest if it departed in any way, good or bad,
from the missionary passion that produced "the great
new fact" of twenty-five years ago--the world Christian movement.

At Bangkok Asians themselves were surprised at
the lack of emotional response on the part of the Western inheritors of the mission machinery, as many (often
legitimate) criticisms were levelled at the classical
(and evangelical) missionary movement. A great part
of the Westerners' mysterious indifference is simply
the fact that the Asian critics stand much closer (and
more sensitively) to the spirit of the missionary movement than do these current churchmen from the West who
for the most part are not evangelicals and who do not
therefore possess the slightest sense of loyalty that
would prompt them to defend the earlier, evangelical-
controlled movement. The Third World leaders at Bangkok may have slightly under-estimated the degree of
dissassociation between present churchmen who manage
the mission apparatus, and the earlier evangelical
leadership which created and long directed that classical machinery.

Thus the Western churchmen turned out to be just
as critical of the old era as the non-Western churchmen. Both groups could easily have joined in flagel-
lating the absent evangelical party. Indeed, to some
great extent many sophisticated Asians trained in
Western schools, may have gotten their critical cues
in the first place from dissassociated (e.g. non-evangelical, non-missionary) Western churchmen. It is no
wonder that some African spokesmen, closer than some
Asians to the recent cutting edge of Western pioneer
missions, stood up in defense of the great urgency for
present-day world mission and evangelism *in the earlier
sense.*

An analysis of the participants at Bangkok would no doubt reveal, on the one hand, immense and thoughtful efforts at fair representation of all the member churches of the WCC, the various ecclesiastical hues in its membership, nationalities, etc., and on the other hand, little structural or psychological awareness of the continued "alive and doing well" existence of the parent evangelical mission movement and the parents' continued interest. In this sense Emilio Castro--part of the Methodist sphere in Latin America--is a much better choice as the new head of the CWME than was Philip Potter, who derives more nearly from an extension of the European state church phenomenon. I am not the first to note the radical difference between Potter's Caribbean church background and that which is common in Latin America, let alone the more typically "gathered-church" evangelical flavor of church life in the fully non-Western "mission fields" of Asia and Africa.

This concept of "proprietary interest" is not unlike the concern a retired pastor has for a church with which he was long associated, perhaps even founded, once the new pastor comes and moves off in all kinds of brand new directions, neglecting earlier emphases. True, in one sense, the retired pastor has "no business poking his nose into things," yet he inevitably feels very much involved emotionally. The analogy is not complete: in America the "new pastor" took 100 years in coming (say, from 1837 to 1937) as centralized *church* leadership gradually took control over formerly evangelical-controlled mission boards loosely associated to the churches (see my *The Warp and the Woof* for a more extensive study of this phenomenon; see also "The New Missions and The Mission of the Church", *International Review of Mission* Jan., 1971).

This great transition was not exactly an evil plot. We have taken great pains to explain why the evangelicals did not control the older churches, and did not generally aspire to do so. It should therefore not be surprising that when the churches took control of the mission machinery the locus of the evangelical movement moved from a virtual monopoly over the old-line machinery to the present evangelical para-church mission sphere. The exception to this

being the work of certain younger, post-Evangelical-
Awakening churches that are still explicitly evangelical. But whether by accident or on purpose, the result for evangelicals has been sensed somehow as at
least a colossal loss and by many as a mean betrayal.
Still, most evangelicals really do not think of the
non-evangelicals as apostates any more than Pentecostals think of non-Pentecostal evangelicals in such
terms. If evangelicals were to meet many of the real
people at Bangkok they would have to acknowledge that
for the most part here was not the worst but the very
best of the non-evangelical church.

This fact is the real basis for hope and for
dialogue. I have elsewhere tried to analyze the latter part of this great transition, in my little book,
The Twenty-Five Unbelievable Years, 1945-1969 (William Carey Library), pointing out the need for a new
variety of *oikoumenical* (not ecumenical) understanding
that would bring peace between the churches on the one
hand and the para-church structures on the other. I
refer to another aspect of this transition in "The
Planting of Younger Missions" (in *Church/Mission Tensions Today*, Moody Press), namely the conversion of
most of the Mott-founded Christian Councils from councils of para-church mission structures to councils of
churches. I am indebted to John V. Taylor of the CMS
for pointing out to me some years ago the subtle structural implication in the change of name from National
Christian Council to National Council of Churches,
although in some cases (India) the structural change
took place without the change of name. The change has
immense practical significance, but is not theologically
sensitive. That good people on both sides of a little-
discussed structural issue ought to be able to sit down
and talk about it seems to me impelling. The discussion at Ghana was too little and too late. The die may
now be cast, but where there is good will there must
be a way.

As already noted, most (but not all) evangelicals
tend to be wary of both churches and even more of
church councils. Not I. Rather, I am convinced that
it is a case of both/and. *Both* churches and para-
church structures must be seen to have an entirely
legitimate, complimentary role--can we not see the

mainly wholesome balance between diocese and order in the Roman tradition?--and I feel that the only way forward today is for a cease-fire between these two kinds of structures, since a continuing tension between structures compounds the already existing tensions between evangelical and non-evangelical. Furthermore, this structural problem is or ought to be pretty nearly non-theological. The CMS has by now weathered all the theological storms of protest, and in so doing should have permanently won the battle for all accountable para-church structures in the protestant tradition.

BEYOND BANGKOK: EDINBURGH II

This line of thinking puts Bangkok into an unusual perspective. As Shepherd shows, Bangkok may be seen as the present-day survival of an organization (the IMC) whose membership once consisted solely of councils of mission agencies, that is, para-church structures, not churches. At Bangkok it is under the new management of a long list of organizations that are strictly churches, churches which may or may not participate in any kind of on-going evangelistic mission. Were there any missionaries at Bangkok? Not very many. I am not speaking only of Western missionaries. The characteristic churchly viewpoint cannot easily conceive of--nor therefore anticipate--the need for non-Western, para-church mission agencies. Yet a recent study (*Missions from the Third World*, Wong, Larson, Pentecost, Church Growth Book Club, South Pasadena, Calif. 91030) has a preliminary total of over 200 non-Western agencies which send more than 3,000 missionaries. As I have pointed out elsewhere[1] para-church structures (whether they be the prestigious Church Mission Society of the Church of England or the immense, world-wide United Bible Societies, or the Billy Graham Evangelistic Association) can have no organic relation to the CWME; they cannot have any official representation at a Bangkok meeting; they are there only if some member church sends them as a delegate or they are appointed in some other category by the CWME staff (e.g. the DWME), which is itself chosen by a mechanism representing churches, not para-church structures. I say this not by way of criticism or

complaint. I doubt if it is feasible to try to roll
back history. The point is simply that there must be
a constructive alternative.

What is Different About Edinburgh II?

In 1790 William Carey, employing the example of
the Catholic mission societies, barely persuaded a
small group of pastors that it was legitimate to or-
ganize something other than a church for the purpose
of organizing churches among "the heathens." As it
turned out, his structural initiative helped to trig-
ger literally dozens of other such societies into existence during the next few years, and precipitated for
Protestantism the functional equivalent of the Catholic
orders, which by that date had a most embarassing 250-yr.
lead on Protestants in the task of world evangelization.
As a truly visionary strategist he then proposed that
people involved in these peculiar, new, non-ecclesiastical "means" for the evangelization of non-Christians
ought to meet together some years hence in a world-wide
gathering in 1810 to compare notes and promote the task.
He was only 100 years ahead of others: what he envisioned did not really come to pass until 1910. And,
tragically, the same kind of meeting has never happened
since.

In June, 1972 another Baptist, Dr. Luther Cope-
land, President of the (U.S.) Association of Professors
of Missions proposed at the annual meeting of the APM
that there be another such conference. Let's call it
Edinburgh II. Harold Lindsell, editor of *Christianity
Today*, whose response to Bangkok is contained in this
book, is also known as a proponent of an Edinburgh II,
and his evaluation of Bangkok is no doubt derived in
part from Bangkok's lack of congruence to that earlier
conference. But there really ought not to be any conflict between the role of a Bangkok-type meeting and
an Edinburgh type of meeting. If evangelicals can
just adjust themselves to the fact that Bangkok, rightly
or wrongly, just isn't Edinburgh, they can get on with
the job of setting up a second Edinburgh.

A sprightly, beautiful thing was the sudden emergence last December (1972) of what was, for the U.S.

region at least, a mini-Edinburgh. There had not been
a meeting of this type since the demise of the Foreign
Missions Conference of North America, some of the older
participants remarked. The electrifying success of
this meeting is proof positive that an Edinburgh II is
eminently feasible: mixed together in warm mutual
understanding at this meeting were old-fashioned mission-
minded people in a gathering that was confessionally
broader than Bangkok, including as it did prominently,
and not in any secondary category, extremely conservative evangelicals, main-line Protestants, Moravians,
Mennonites and Roman Catholics.

How in the world did evangelicals quite willingly
collaborate in this gathering? Was it because it was
not officially sponsored by the National Council of
Churches of Christ in the USA? Yes, and no. Many well-
known NCC-related people were there, prominently, and
this was known in advance. Quite a few at this meeting met again a few days later at Bangkok. How did
evangelicals in fair numbers get invited to this meet-
ing--and go--when at Bangkok they were not invited, and
mainly would not have gone had they been invited?

Very simple. The December, 1972 Chicago "Consultation on Frontier Missions" was not sponsored officially by any church or council of churches, *nor was
any person there sent by a church body as such*. It was,
as was Edinburgh 1910, a consultation built from representatives of para-church agencies of mission, or denominational mission boards. It may seem like a small
point (yet it clearly makes a big difference), but it
is a fact that neither at Edinburgh 1910 nor at Chicago
1972 were any ecclesiastical offices as such asked to
send any participants. Naturally everyone present was
a member of some church, but the wider-than-Bangkok
ecclesiastical spectrum was virtually accidental, the
reason being that if you invite mission agencies of all
kinds to send participants to a consultation, you inevitably get people whose "employment" is in those
para-church structures, yes, but whose "citizenship" is
in dozens of different churches, probably a wider spectrum than can be gathered at an official church-sponsored consultation. Thus, what I am saying is not
really very hypothetical. The Chicago meeting is now

a fact of history, documented by a 400-page book, *The Gospel and Frontier Peoples*, edited by R. Pierce Beaver ($3.25 postpaid from the William Carey Library, South Pasadena, Calif.). There is absolutely no reason that kind of meeting can't happen again. Indeed, so many things turned out beyond expectations that the continuation committee is enthusiastically looking forward to the next one.

It is clear that evangelicals readily mix with all kinds of people in non-ecclesiastical and non-conciliar encounters. Prominent evangelicals from the strictest quarters are represented in the newly-founded American Society of Missiology right along with old-line Protestants and Roman Catholics from many different orders. Why? Not because there is a limp, watered-down creedal requirement for membership, but *because there is none at all*.

Evangelicals, as we have seen, are exceedingly wary of ecclesiastical tyranny. Their freedom is hard won. Even the National Association of Evangelicals in the U.S. is relatively small--less than four million, while its service agencies serve 20 million! Evangelicals will stay away--and criticize--when the meeting looks too ecclesiastical. Their unity is "fellowship in service," organically undefined. The distinction between a Bangkok, controlled by churches, and an Edinburgh that is a free association of people from parachurch structures, is all-important.

But Isn't Edinburgh Out of Date?

At this point some readers will be desperately tired of all this talk. They will admit there was a meeting at Chicago and that there could be a second Edinburgh. Their screaming questions are "But why do it? Aren't missions out of date? Haven't we all agreed--at least at Bangkok--that the 19th century missionary era is over?" "Your own organization," they tell me (referring to COEMAR, UPCUSA) "did away with the very word *missionary*! You were yourself in more recent years a 'fraternal worker', not a missionary. How can you forget all this as you write?"

I have not forgotten. I am still thrilled by the
keen thinking behind this new terminology, and totally
supportive of it. Missions and missionaries *are* out
of date--always have been--*in regard to the flow of
workers, fraternally, from one church to another*. There
must be a massive disengagement of all missionary-style
workers from relationships with sister churches. This
is one "great new fact" concomitant to the other "great
new fact" of the emergence of the non-Western churches.
And granted that not everyone yet quite understands
the significance of this welcome, long-overdue clarification, let us be equally clear that the desirable
disengagement of true missionaries from church-to-church
relationships *says absolutely nothing at all about any
lessening need for missions and missionaries*!

Fraternal workers go where there are churches
already. They go humbly to work under the authority of
the receiving churches. They should be part of a perma-
nent two-way flow. Missionaries go where there are no
churches, where there is no authority under which to
work other than the mission that sends them. Churchmen
at a Bangkok-type meeting are concerned, as church leaders properly are concerned, about their own constituencies, and the vitality of the work and witness of those
constituencies in their immediate contexts. Missionaries
have their eyes fixed, not on believers and their community in Christ, but upon the "two billion" who do not
believe. Churchmen may talk about the church-in-mission,
but they are likely talking about the role of a community
of believers, not about the reaching of a community of
non-believers. Churchmen start with bodies of believers
and yearn to lift these brethren higher. Missionaries
start with multitudes of unbelievers and yearn to bring
them into the first few steps of belief. The "children"
of the churchmen and fraternal workers are teenagers
that need to learn social responsibilities; the "children" the missionary seeks are yet to be born. The parents
of teenagers may have forgotten where babies come from,
and the labor pains of birth are forgotten memories.
Few of the participants at Bangkok had had any personal
experience in starting a new church, or in working across
cultural boundaries with totally non-Christian people.
An Edinburgh II would be very different--there would not
be leaders of churches present but leaders of missions

(whether or not church-related). If the distinction
between church-to-church operations and mission-to-
mission operations were maintained, few if any representatives would be present from even the "mission
boards" of the WCC member churches. Many Asian churches
would have not even a department that could send a
single delegate. The meeting would have to build upon
strictly those active agencies involved in extending
the Gospel to the non-Christian majority of our world
today. That would be--will be--a very different kind
of gathering from Bangkok. This observation does not
in itself cast the slightest aspersions upon Bangkok.
In one sense it underlines the distinctive contribution of what Bangkok might have been had it not become
an exclusively church-sponsored affair, but its main
thrust is to suggest the enduring relevance of Edinburgh.

But Was Edinburgh Valid in the First Place?

"Statistically you may be right," some will say,
"there are 2 billion non-Christians. It is true, statistically, that there are more Hindus today than when
the first missionaries went to India. We now have a
new perspective, and the very idea of missionaries converting Hindus is repulsive." Dialogue, it is said,
must *replace*, not merely *augment*, traditional methods.
The German delegate's response to Thailand's Watakeecharoen (p. 64) reflects this perspective.

From this standpoint it is not merely a question
of whether or not new conditions (e.g., the world church,
nationalism, etc.) require a new non-missionary approach,
a Bangkok instead of an Edinburgh. The question here is
whether or not the Edinburgh-type of conversion-missions
ever were proper. Since this is basically an old question on which much is written, (Alan Tippett deals with
it in a new way in *Verdict Theology in Missionary Theory*,
William Carey Library, p. 37ff.), let us merely note that
the dialogue on dialogue-vs-conversion mainly overlooks
the extensive and scholarly discussion, by anthropologically trained missionary thinkers, of the concept of a
completely non-imperialistic cross-cultural diffusion of
faith. Charles Kraft's article, "Dynamic Equivalence

Churches" in the January 1973 issue of *Missiology, An International Review* (Vol I, No. 1), published by the American Society of Missiology, is just one recent example of this kind of scholarly inquiry that renders much of the discussion about missionary aggression obsolete. Here is where there is likely a wide disparity in reading habits between the two groups.

The validity of an Edinburgh is not easily evaluated by people disassociated from the subject. Scholarly missionary discussion such as has been found in the nineteen-year-old journal, *Practical Anthropology* (now merged into the new *Missiology* mentioned just above) is relatively unknown among churchmen. There are two different agendas. Bangkok participants' journal subscriptions are a different set from those of the people who would be prominent at an Edinburgh II, just as the content of the *International Review of Mission* is now very different from the original *International Review of Missions* (note the final *s*). The change of name (by dropping the final *s*) was long in coming, discreetly done, and entirely logical. It could have been done abruptly at the time the IMC was voted into the structure of the WCC at New Delhi. Actually, as we have seen, the IMC had already greatly changed, and in some ways it could have been done earlier. The new *IRM* (no *s*) is logically concerned about the entire "mission" of the church, not just some of the missions of the church. Everyone must certainly agree that the broad mission of the people of God cannot be confined to classical cross-cultural conversion missions. But does the latter lose its validity once the broader concept is enunciated?

The appearance of the new journal *Missiology, an International Review* ($8 per year, 135 N. Oakland, Pasadena, Calif.) is evidence that quite a few people feel the role of the older *IRM* (with an *s*) is still quite valid. Had Bangkok decided to kill the *IRM*--as was debated--the American Society of Missiology would have negotiated for the use of the older name. Any similarity between the ASM's *MIR* (as above) and the CWME's *IRM* is not accidental, but then the launching of the *MIR* is not in any sense competitive: the new

MIR hopes to pick up the task of the old *IRM*, not the new *IRM*! Perhaps this new burst of energy in the ASM and its new *MIR*, combining, as it does, so very broad a spectrum of Christian traditions, will help illumi- nate this ultimate questioning of the original (not just present-day) validity of the classical missions. Perhaps we must finally confess our dependence upon specifically missionary scholars rather than churchmen- theologians or even "fraternal worker" scholars. Church- men tend to live within the world view of their own church. The fraternal worker tends to live within the world view of a foreign church. Only the missionary, by our definition, is preoccupied by the world of unbelief, its nature, its potentiality, its future.

Where would we be without the thinking of such missionary scholars as Kraemer, Freytag, Bavinck, Zwe- mer, Vicedom, Luzbetak, Newbigin, Maurier, etc.? We look forward eagerly to writings from non-Western mis- sionaries, too--Samuel Kim, for example, who was at Chicago 1972 and is a Korean who has worked 17 years in Thailand.

Those who question the validity of an Edinburgh II will not likely be interested in "Lausanne 1974", the International Congress on World-wide Evangelization, promoted by one of the large para-church evangelism organizations absent at Bangkok, the Billy Graham Evan- gelistic Association, and sponsored by a one-hundred- man committee that unconsciously mixes both churchmen and mission leaders. July of 1974 is only weeks away, and the unfolding plans are a vast, creatively orches- trated phenomenon. The avowed interest of the planners is to emphasize for Christians around the world E1, E2, and E3 evangelism, a completely non-geographical scheme: E1 is evangelism among people of one's own language and culture wherever they may be found. E2 is evangelism among people (again, wherever they may be found) who are culturally near, yet sufficiently distant (culturally) to be unlikely to join the ecclesiastical tradition of the evangelistic worker. E3 evangelism is work among people (near or far geographically) who are culturally totally strange to the worker.

Functionally this great meeting (3,000 are being invited) may be much closer to an Edinburgh II than anything on a world level thus far. Chicago 1972 was re-
gional. The Berlin Congress on Evangelism in 1966 was
not at all clearly focussed on the totally unreached
peoples of the world. Both Berlin and Bangkok shared
the desperately naive concept that now that there are
Christians in every land, foreign-language-learning missionaries are no longer required. The overwhelming truth
is that most of the two billion non-Christians are either
E2 or E3 distances away from existing Christian communities: stress on back-door evangelism, the expansion of
existing churches is a totally inadequate strategy.

Lausanne 1974 will go beyond this. How far? The
planning machinery is very receptive to suggestions.
But it will not truly be an Edinburgh II because there
will be no *delegates*, just invited participants. The
eight unique features on Latourette's famous list are
not all equally significant, but the first two are surely
essential:[2] 1) "it was strictly a *delegated* body, made
up of official representatives of missionary societies"
(what we here would call E2 and E3 para-church organizations), and 2) "it was a deliberative body, seeking to
formulate policy for the years ahead. While it possessed
no legislative authority, it could suggest, and because
it was composed of leaders of the various societies there
was reason to suppose that its recommendations would be
followed by action."

Lausanne 1974 will surely throw additional light on
the dimensions of the task remaining in world evangelization. Many vital by-products may come from this project
meeting. One of them, one of the most important, may be
Edinburgh II.

———

1. Ralph D. Winter, *The Twenty-Five Unbelievable Years,
    1945-1969*. South Pasadena, Calif.: William Carey
    Library, 1969, pp. 68, 69.

2. Kenneth Scott Latourette, *A History of Christianity*.
    New York: Harper and Row, 1953, pp. 1343, 1344.

PART I

Pre-Bangkok Anticipations

SALVATION TODAY

Donald A. McGavran

The Central Committee of the World Council of Churches has issued a call for a world-wide conference on the theme, Salvation Today. The gathering will be held in Bangkok from December 29th to January 21st, 1973. It will be an expensive meeting, drawing in men and women from all over the world to consider one crucial question:

*What is the salvation which
Jesus Christ offers men today?*

It is highly significant that, while the mission aim of the World Council of Churches, and indeed of all Churches of Christ, is "to further the proclamation of the Gospel to all men that they may believe and be saved," all the advance publications concerning this meeting indicate that the World Council is making a massive effort to reinterpret the classic meaning of that aim so that 'being saved' will come to mean having more food, more justice, more clothes, more freedom, more production, less disease, more brotherhood, more peace, in short, <u>more this-worldly</u> improvements.

Dr. Donald A. McGavran is the Dean Emeritus of the School of World Mission and Institute of Church Growth at Fuller Theological Seminary. He is the apostle of the Church Growth School of thought.

A United Methodist minister writing me under date of June 28th, 1972, puts the issue succinctly:

> My friends on the left are always saying to me that we Evangelicals should remember that it is both personal salvation <u>and social action</u>. But when I go to Methodist Convocations and read materials from our Board of Missions, I want to stand up and say, "Brethren, please remember it is both social concern <u>and personal salvation</u>." My brethren to the left so infrequently remember the advice they are so free to give me.

Precisely this issue will underlie the Bangkok Gathering. Advance W.C.C. materials insist (on Old Testament grounds) that "salvation" has primarily to do with the current life of flesh and blood, hunger and satiation, manufacturing and distributing, freedom and wholeness <u>in this world</u>.

We hope and pray that as the meeting takes place, better counsels will prevail. We trust that delegates will insist that the Old Testament passages must not be taken by themselves. They alone do not represent the whole biblical revelation. They must be understood also in the light of the unity of the Bible and seen also in the light of the New Testament revelation.

The magnitude of the truncated, sub-biblical deviation being proposed is seen in the fact that all Branches of the Christian Church in all ages have held and all Christians have believed that salvation in the Christian sense means primarily the salvation of the soul which results in abundant life in the body. Such eternal salvation is the most effective agent of temporal peace and righteousness. The possession of this salvation enables the saved to enter into the cultural task to which God calls His people.

The Old Testament is one long recital of all kinds of
temporal improvements which God gave His people in the
course of disclosing Himself to them as their Redeemer.
It says, "God saved His people in these ways, binding
them in covenant to be His people and abide in His laws."
However, all such improvements (destruction of enemies,
abundance of food, riches, status, multitudes of children,
houses and vineyards, horses and chariots) turned out to
be temporary palliatives. God took the Hebrews - strictly
bound to worship Him only - to a land flowing with milk
and honey, and lo, within a short time they were disobey-
ing Him, worshipping the baals and asherah, committing
adulteries under every green tree, and grinding the
faces of the poor!! He forgave them and gave them David's
Kingdom. Within one generation, kings, priests, and
people had with enthusiasm abandoned the religion of Yah-
weh for that of the prestigious gods of the land. During
all these centuries it became clear that until the heart
of man is changed, until he is saved through faith in
Jesus Christ and becomes a new creature, until he is
firmly joined to the Body and continues in the means of
grace, no amount of milk and honey (more to eat and wear,
better houses, more justice, more peace, greater individual and national income) is of lasting value.

The issue at Bangkok is clear: does the word salvation,
according to the Bible, mean eternal salvation or does
it mean this-worldly improvements? Which is the basic
meaning? It appears as if the conciliar forces are set to
maintain, on the basis of the Old Testament, that salvation means primarily if not exclusively this-worldly improvements. Evangelicals will maintain, on the basis of
the total biblical record (the New Testament as well as
the Old) that 'salvation' means a change in status of the
soul, the essential person, is achieved through faith in
Jesus Christ alone, and results in abundant life in this
world.

"Once you were no people, but now you are God's people."
(1 Pet. 2:10) "If you confess with your lips that
Jesus is Lord and believe in your heart that God

raised Him from the dead, you will be saved." (Romans
10:9) "There is salvation in no one else, for there
is no other name under heaven given among men by which
we must be saved." (Acts 4:12)

Let us note what the debate is <u>not</u> about, i.e. what is
agreed on. Both conciliar and non-conciliar Christians
agree that temporal improvements in man's lot (both individual and social) are desirable. On biblical grounds
both agree that Christians should do good to all men,
that the hungry should be fed, the naked should be clothed,
those in prison should be visited, justice should roll
down like waters, and righteousness as a mighty stream.
Agreed. Furthermore, it is agreed that a considerable
part of the Church's treasure should be spent to achieve
these good temporal ends. Missions in the past hundred
years have spent from a half to nine-tenths of their men
and money for education, medicine, agricultural improvement, and the like. The proportion of the whole budget
spent for these things is always a matter for debate, but
that a substantial amount be so spent is seldom questioned.
No one is advocating that since God grants salvation to
those who believe on Christ and are incorporated in His
Church, nothing further is required. On the contrary,
Christians continually insist that the saved while they
are in this world, must and will live in forgiveness and
love and press on toward righteousness and justice. Disagreement does not lie on these points.

Disagreement lies in whether temporal improvements are
salvation or a fruit of the saved life. The distinction
is vitally important. Bangkok will not be splitting hairs.
If 'salvation today' means political liberation, land
distribution, better pay for factory workers, the down-
fall of oppressive systems of government, and the like,
then the whole apparatus of missions is rightfully used
to achieve these ends. Evangelism will be downgraded.
Churching the unchurched will be neglected and ridiculed.
The airplane of missions will be diverted away from the
propagation of the Gospel to the establishment of utopias.

Indeed, these emphases have been occurring during the last fifteen years. "Salvation" is the fourth word which the World Council of Churches is reinterpreting. All are being devalued in the same direction. Their eternal significance is being minimized and their temporal meanings underlined.

a) "Mission" ceases to be the propagation of the Gospel
    and becomes everything God wants done by Christians
    or non-Christians - which necessarily limits what
    what God wants done to the field of ethics.

b) "Evangelism" ceases to be proclaiming Jesus Christ
    by word and deed and persuading men to become His
    disciples and responsible members of His Church
    and becomes changing the structures of society in
    the direction of justice, righteousness and peace.

c) "Conversion" ceases to be turning from idols to
    serve the God and Father of our Lord Jesus Christ,
    as revealed in the Bible, and becomes turning cor-
    porately from faulty social configurations to those
    which liberate men and incorporate them in the great
    brotherhood.

d) "Salvation" is apparently going to be put through
    the same rolling mill and brought out flattened and
    focused on temporal improvements.

    (One kind friend urged me to concede that my bifocals
    - without which I cannot read or write - are an im-
    portant part of my salvation!)

Evangelicals should work and pray that this deliberate debasing of Christian currency cease and that the reformation of the social order (rightly emphasized) should not be substituted for salvation. Salvation is something which the true and living God confers on His creatures in accordance with His once-for-all revelation in Jesus Christ, God and Saviour according to the Bible. Salvation is a vertical relationship (of man with God) which issues in horizontal relationships (of man with men). The vertical must not be displaced by the horizontal.

Desirable as social ameliorations are, working for them must not be substituted for the biblical requirements of/for 'salvation'. Those requirements are clear: The New Testament states them again and again. Paul voiced them in their simplest form to the Philippian jailer: "Believe in the Lord Jesus, and you will be saved, you and your household." (Acts 16:31)

Church Growth Bulletin hopes that three agreements will come out of Bangkok and urges readers to work and pray that such may eventuate. Let us all agree -

1. That beyond question the Bible teaches that God's people ought continually and creatively to work for a just, brotherly, righteous and peaceful order in their families, neighborhoods, states, world.

2. That beyond question the Bible teaches that to become God's people it is necessary for all men (descendents of Christians and non-Christians alike) to believe on Jesus Christ as Lord and Saviour, receive Him in their hearts, receive Him in their hearts, become responsible members of His Church, and manifest the fruits of the Spirit in their lives. And that this alone may rightly be called 'salvation today'.

3. That, in consequence, it is desirable for the Church to press forward with classic Christian mission (proclaiming Christ by word and deed and persuading men to become His disciples and responsible members of His Church) on the one hand, and with a program of social action and humanitarian concern on the other. Christians should be entirely free to support each program according to their conscience. It is unacceptable for leaders of missionary societies to determine to what kind of missions they will devote the givings of the devout. Donors themselves must decide whether they wish to carry on 'making disciples' or 'reforming society!

2

A look at Bangkok
in historical perspective

Where did the Bangkok conference on "Salvation Today" come from? Jack Shepherd's answer to that question is not just a dry collection of historical facts, but it bristles with incisive analysis. Here is an evangelical interpretation of the recent ecumenical history that led to Bangkok.

JACK F. SHEPHERD

The purpose of this article about the recent "Salvation Today" conference is to attempt to react to it in the perspective of its own particular history. The brochure describing the conference program, and at least three other things written in anticipation of Bangkok, have sought to establish a continuity and development from Edinburgh, 1910 to Bangkok, 1972-73.

This same approach of pleading a case on the basis of a claim to historical succession is a familiar one to those of us who have read from the literature of the ecumenical movement. For example, the preparatory booklet for New Delhi advocated the integration of the International Missionary Council into the World Council of Churches in much the same way. The fine series of Bible studies on Witness, Service and Unity were supplemented with the defining of New Delhi developments as fulfillment of a half-century of the ecumenical process. (The chart from the booklet is a useful one and is included here.)

The inaugural Assembly of the Commission on World Mission and Evangelism occurred in conjunction with the Third Assembly of WCC in New Delhi in 1961. Constitutional provision for merger was made at the Ghana Assembly of the

Jack F. Shepherd is the Education Secretary of the Christian and Missionary Alliance. He was serving as a missionary in China when forced to leave because of Communist pressure, and subsequently he served the Christian and Missionary Alliance in the Philippines. A noted author and speaker, one of his most recent contributions is a chapter entitled, "Is the Church Really Necessary?" in the symposium, *Church/Mission Tensions Today* (Moody).

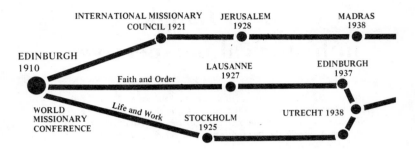

International Missionary Council, which was held in Accra, Ghana, December 28, 1957 — January 8, 1958. The CWME with its own division staff within the WCC became "in all respects" the successor of the IMC. However, a committee report from New Delhi makes clear that a broadening of the scope of the Commission's Mandate for Mission was envisioned. "Our temptation will be to think of the Division simply as the continuation of the interests of the International Missionary Council with emphasis on Asia, Africa and South America. We must resist this temptation. This is the Division of World Mission and Evangelism of the World Council of Churches. We are concerned not with three continents but with six" (*The New Delhi Report*, 1961, Constitution of the CWME, p. 250).

A full meeting of the CWME was convened two years after the New Delhi Assembly in Mexico City in 1963. "Witness to Six Continents" was a key theme and was the title of the official report of the conference. As will be noted, the big question on the Bangkok agenda was formulated at Mexico City: "What is the form and content of the salvation which Christ offers men in the secular world?" (*Occasional Bulletin*, Volume XXII, No. 13, 1971).

My purpose is to dissent from a commendatory and optimistic interpretation of this history, but before I make critical charges of discontinuity and deviation, let me acknowledge my inclination to agree with the wording of the stated Aim of the CWME and the doctrinal Basis of the WCC. The editor of the *International Review of Missions* raised the Bangkok question in announcing the prospective conference (Volume LXII, No. 228, October '68):

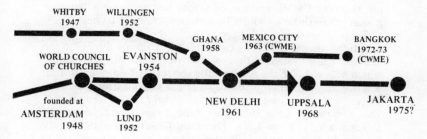

When the International Missionary Council was integrated into the World Council of Churches at New Delhi, 1961, as the Commission on World Mission and Evangelism, it acquired an explicit *Aim*: 'To further the proclamation to the whole world of the Gospel of Jesus Christ to the end that all men may believe in Him and be saved.' At the same time the World Council revised its *Basis* to make more explicit the dynamic nature of the ecumenical movement: 'The World Council of Churches is a fellowship of churches which confess the Lord Jesus Christ as God and Saviour according to the Scriptures and therefore seek to fulfill together their common calling to the glory of the one God, Father, Son and Holy Spirit.' The operative words here are *Savior* and *saved*. What do they mean? They and their cognates do not occur very frequently in the New Testament, but they are often used to define the purpose of Christ's mission to the pagan world.

Most evangelicals would agree on the definition of those "operative words" and the stated aim and basis for that matter. Moreover, we recognize that many in ecumenical circles are committed to the same essential evangelical faith as we are. However, the apprehension and even antagonism of many of us toward ecumenical trends may prove to be justified when the outcome of Bangkok becomes apparent. This paper is being written prior to the conference. Perhaps its critical and apprehensive outlook will have been wrong. Let us hope so.

I do not agree with the interpretation that heralds Bangkok as a fulfillment of a missionary purpose derived from Edinburgh and its antecedents. On the contrary, I wonder if Bangkok is not, in fact, committing itself primarily to a sort of social and development program. However, if such an enterprise, however laudatory, becomes a substitute for the "salvation" that has been consistently defined in clear biblical terms from Edinburgh on, then the CWME and the WCC may be proclaiming "another gospel" than those to whose history they claim to be heirs.

It is illustrative to suggest that "the uncertainty about salvation" theme is the logical result of two prior threats to the call for "the evangelization of the world in this generation" which was right at the heart of the concerns of Edinburgh from whence the movement for ecumenical organization has been derived (cf. *The Evangelization of the World in this Generation: The Resurgence of a Missionary Idea Among the Conservative Evangelicals*, Denton Lotz, Hamburg Dissertation, 1970). My reading of this history is in three stages which may climax in Bangkok in an abandonment, not a realization, of what began at Edinburgh. I want to offer brief explanation of what I see as three unfortunate phases of compromising ecumenical developments:

1. First, there was the unfortunate distraction from world missions to church unification.

2. Then there was the subordinating assimilation of mission into ecclesiastical bureaucracy.

3. Inevitably, we seem to have come to a complete confusion of the church's unique saving mission with any helpful service given to a needy world.

I. Two Movements Arising Out of Edinburgh

Any diagram of ecumenical development such as the one alluded to above will draw at least two lines out from Edinburgh. The one most familiar to conservative evangelicals sets out as the first major event the founding of the International Missionary Council in 1921. Then, the five IMC conferences are spaced along the line: Jerusalem '28, Madras '38, Whitby '47, Willingen '52 and Ghana '58.

It is very important to note that parallel to the line of movement for world mission is the line that leads to Amsterdam '48 and the formation of the World Council of Churches.

Now it must be acknowledged that there were those who served on both sides of the dichotomous situation discerning the necessity of simultaneous development of church and mission. If non-conciliar missions people had done their homework on the history of these two parallel movements, we would be better able to handle the church-mission tensions we are now finding so urgent.

Having admitted that there were elements of sound logic and

biblical fidelity in the correlation of these two streams from Edinburgh, I want to claim that the movement toward organizational church union became a distraction and deviation from the central purpose of Edinburgh. It resulted not only in the alienation of conservative evangelicals (cf. Lotz, 1970), but it also, in my judgment, blurred the great IMC vision of mission.

One aspect of the diminution of the biblical understanding of mission is evident in the bifurcation of the church unification line into another two lines — Faith and Order and Life and Work. Compromise was incipient in this combination as evidenced in such expressions as "doctrine divides, service unites". How much did Stockholm '25 (Life and Work) and Lausanne '27 (Faith and Order) affect Jerusalem '28? The same pattern was present in the relation of Oxford '37 and Edinburgh '37 to Madras '38. Then, Whitby, trying to regroup for "partnership in obedience" in mission, was surely overshadowed by the unveiling of the World Council of Churches at Amsterdam in '48. As could be expected, there was the convergence of the two divergent lines from Edinburgh in New Dehli '61 in the integration of IMC and WCC.

II. Mission Identity Lost in the Structure?

The conservative evangelical perspective on the history of the ecumenical movement highlights a second danger and defect. In spite of the high ideals and beautiful theological formulations that people like Bishop Newbigin have brought to the support of the integration of "mission and church," hopes have not been fulfilled nor real progress made toward genuine "renewal in mission."

The moving introductory statement of the Report of the Third Assembly Committee on the CWME is quoted here. In reading it one must ask, "Have the past ten years given evidence that the great promise of it has been realized?" I fear not. It seems on the contrary that there has even been a tragic lack of faithfulness to it.

The integration of the International Missionary Council and the World Council of Churches brings into being a new instrument of common consultation and action to serve the Churches in their missionary task under the new conditions of the second half of the twentieth century. In it we see the good hand of God leading us into the next phase of the Church's mission. It is at the same time a fitting symbol of the fact that missionary responsibility cannot be separated from any other aspect of the Church's life and teaching. The Christian mission is one throughout the world, for there is but one Gospel of salvation for all men, one Saviour and Lord, who is the light of the world . . .

As we face the new situation, we are at the same time heirs of the spiritual riches of the missionary movement of past centuries. The very existence of a World Council of Churches is a sign of God's blessing upon that movement . . . Integration must mean that the World Council of Churches takes the missionary task into the very heart of its life, and also that the missionary agencies of the churches place their work in an ecumenical perspective and accept whatever new insights God may give through new relationships.

The missionary task is not finished. It is rather entering upon a new and more challenging phase. All our concerns with one another must not cause us to forget the fact that two-thirds of the human race are without the knowledge of Christ as the light of the world. We owe them that knowledge. We have no better claim to Christ than they have. Nothing else that we can offer them is a discharge of that debt.

The calling of God to his Church today is for a new offering of life. For some, especially among the youth of the churches, it is a call for life-long missionary service abroad. For all of every age, and out of every nation, it is a call to total and unconditional commitment to the mission of God . . . (The New Dehli Report, p. 249).

The real issue is, What was "that mission" to which New Delhi called for commitment? It would not be fair or accurate to say that the idea of mission became ambiguous or that mission lost its identity just because it was assimilated organizationally into the WCC structure. However, the results of this particular institutional integration of church and mission are such as to give comfort to those of us who keep calling for a separateness of church and mission. I will not attempt to argue the case for structures here. I do, however, want to make one more comment on the situation that prevailed when it could be said "the church *is* mission" or mission is "everything the church does outside its four walls." This kind of immobilizing imprecision elicited the classic, but prophetic, lament, "If everything is mission, pretty soon nothing is mission."

I want to note the erosion of the idea of the church's unique, saving mission in two stages between New Dehli and Bangkok. Then, in conclusion, I want to try to point out that having perilously generalized the missionary function, the more recent developments have introduced serious uncertainty about the very message of Jesus Christ as Savior.

No thoughtful person should quarrel with the emphasis at

Mexico City on "Mission in Six Continents". However, the meaning of mission was beclouded in the CWME debate that Thomas Wieser reports on:

> The discussion raised a theological issue which remained unresolved. Debate returned again and again to the relationship between God's action in and through the church and everything God is doing in the world apparently independently of the Christian community. Can a distinction be drawn between God's providential action and God's redeeming action? If the restoration and reconciliation of human life is being achieved by the action of God through secular human agencies, what is the place and significance of faith? If the church is to be wholly involved in the world and its history, what is the true nature of its separateness? We were able to state the thesis and antithesis in this debate, but we could not see our way through to the truth which we feel lies beyond this dialectic (*Occasional Bulletin*, Volume XXII, No. 13, 1971).

How can the missionary obligation and function of the church be kept clear at all, if the distinction between the church and the world is fuzzed out? If the church is, as was affirmed at Willingen, God's "instrument for mission," is its service to the world not primarily redemptive?

The Mexico City uncertainties came through loud and strong at Uppsala, with such supporting documents as *Planning for Mission* and *The Church for Others*. This story, including some of its sad notes, has been told in other places. It is sufficient here to observe that Section II of the Fourth Assembly Report seems to say that mission is a myth, rather than to provide, as it professes to do, "a mandate for mission." John Coventry Smith was surely right when he said in his appeal for acceptance of the final draft of "Renewal in Mission", "There is at this time no common understanding of the nature and limitations of the Christian mission or of the method of its implementation" (The Uppsala Report, 1968, p. 38).

III. Ambiguity About The Salvation Proclamation

Verkuyl and Wieser both note that the selection of the Bangkok theme grew out of the Mexico City debate. What seems to me an unfaithful step was taken in proposing that a better definition of "the form and content of the salvation which Christ offers men" than the Bible provides might be discovered. As Wieser said, "In trying to answer this question, we must not only clarify the biblical and theological meaning of the salvation in Christ, but we need to pay closer attention to the great diversity of contemporary experience and to the many ways in which the need and the search, but sometimes also the promise of salvation, is being expressed in the midst of that diversity."

The material gathered together in an attempt to understand the contemporary experience of salvation is fascinating and useful. The unfortunate thing is that it appears that some of these claims and notions are regarded as having the same validity and authority as biblical truth about salvation. If we are reluctant about the combination of Scripture *and tradition as* sources of authority, we should be even more wary of Scripture *and* contemporary experience as authoritative. We must not give up on "salvation talk" that is based on the Bible, even if it does seem to "remain meaningless for many people" (*Occasional Bulletin, op. cit.*).

The clouds of ambiguity remained after Uppsala. Visser 't Hooft spoke a wistful word about the mandate of the ecumenical movement as he had heard it enunciated by Bishop Soderblom in Uppsala Cathedral in 1925. It involved, he said, "one task with two aspects: to manifest the oneness of the people of God and to enable it to witness with a common voice to the full gospel of salvation with its definite implications for the world (*Report*, p. 314). Uppsala did not seem to hear.

These two points from Soderblom remind one in a striking way of the climatic passage in Visser 't Hooft's little book, *No Other Name*, (SCM, London, 1963). It is appropriate to this discussion to note that the title is taken from Acts 4:12, that crucial salvation text. It is also to be noted that he speaks here of the "New Humanity" theme, five years before Uppsala featured it.

If Bangkok participants are really loyal to their own history, they might well test their profession and experience of "salvation" by the great word of their own doughty, ecumenical statesman, Visser 't Hooft. In coming to his statement of the church's one task in two aspects, he affirms his faith in "Christian universalism." He surely explains what "Salvation Today" is in the series of passages from which the following selections have been made:

Let us try to describe the nature of that specific universalism which is rooted in the Gospel.

It has its source and foundation in one person: Jesus Christ . . . In every part of the New Testament, in every stage of the early tradition, we find that the coming of Jesus Christ has completely transformed the human situation. Man's eternal destiny depends on his decision concerning the relationship to this one Jesus of Nazareth. It is because of him that the whole outlook for the future has changed. It is through him that a totally new community is formed . . .

He has come at a particular moment of history. He enters into the life of humanity . . .

Since Christ died for all, all have died (II Corinthians 5:15). That is to say: the old humanity is passe, antiquated. The time of the new creation, the new humanity, has come. The meaning of the age in which we live now is that the work of reconciliation which was begun in Christ must still be completed. There are those who have understood what God has done and who accept gratefully the gift of reconciliation. There are those who do not accept and those who have not yet heard the good news. So the word 'all' is now used in two different connotations. Paul says: 'The same Lord is Lord of all', that is to say of the whole of humanity, but he continues: 'and bestows his riches upon all who call upon him' (Romans 10:12), that is to say on those who fulfill the one condition of responding to the good news. As men take their decision for or against him a distinction arises between those who realize the crucial significance of God's deed in Christ and those who do not . . .

This means that the universal Church has as such a double function. First of all it must in its own life manifest the universality which characterizes the new reconciled humanity . . .

The second function of the universal Chruch is to be the messenger of God's universal offer of reconciliation. The 'all', who are one in Christ, exist for the sake of the 'all' for whom Christ died, but who do not know or acknowledge him. The appeal which God makes to humanity is made through ambassadors, through 'us' (II Corinthians 5:20) . . . The divine act on which reconciliation depends has happened once for all and is unrepeatable, but the ministry of reconciliation is to go on till the end of time. The Church is the missionary Church because it is the instrument of God's world-embracing plan of salvation (pp. 100-102).

That luminous statement of universal salvation in Christ seems to me to echo affirmations that have been maintained throughout the history of the ecumenical movement. To be sure, such a view has been questioned and denied, but it seems to me never to have been quite so threatened with betrayal as in the house of Edinburgh's professed friends at Bangkok. I sincerely hope that what I write turns out to be wrong.

3

CONCEPTUAL DYADS IN THE ETHNOTHEOLOGY OF "SALVATION TODAY"

by A. R. TIPPETT *

Margaret Mead, in *Culture and Commitment*, insists that the new question of our day is, "Can I commit my life to anything ? Is there anything in human cultures as they exist today worth saving, worth committing my life to ?" She includes belief in God, in science, in society, in anything at all. It is the question man faces when confronted with "the responsibility of not destroying the human race". I latch on to the word "commit" rather than to the pessimism of the question. My own commitment is to Christian mission in a world that is ready for it. I hope the Bangkok discussions will feel the mood of lands with open doors for people movements, rather than those where the Church is static. I am also committed to a belief in both moral and scientific values, and stand with Horowitz, who says in *Professing Sociology*, "the presence of moral components does not prevent a scientific view of society, but, to the contrary, is *its necessary condition*" [1] (italics mine). Such a commitment is required in missionary anthropology in this new era of rapid cultural change.

Anthropology and Christian Mission

An increasing literature on certain sub-sections of applied anthropology — educational, medical and missionary anthropology [2] — indicate a significant attitudinal shift among anthropologists. Once applied anthropology of any kind had to fight for existence. The study of man was

---

* Dr. TIPPETT is Professor of Missionary Anthropology at the School of World Mission, Fuller Theological Seminary, California. He is a minister of the Australian Methodist Church and did missionary service in the Fiji Islands. He also did research for the WCC in the Solomon Islands in 1964.

[1] HOROWITZ, IRVING LOUIS, *Professing Sociology : Studies in the Life Cycle of Social Science*, Chicago, Aldine Publishing Co. 1968.

[2] Missionary anthropology is covered by such works as : SMALLEY, WM. A. (Ed.), *Readings in Missionary Anthropology*, New York, Practical Anthropology, 1967 ; NIDA, EUGENE A., *Customs and Cultures : Anthropology for Christian Missions*, New York, Harper & Row, 1954 ; *Message and Mission : The Communication of the Christian Faith*, New York, Harper & Bros. Publishers, 1960 ; SMITH, GORDON H., *The Missionary and Anthropology*, Chicago, Moody Press, 1945 ; LAW, HOWARD W., *Winning a Hearing : An Introduction to Missionary Anthropology Linguistics*, Grand Rapids, Wm. B. Eerdmans Pub. Co., 1968 ; and LUZBETAK, LOUIS J., *The Church and Cultures : An Applied Anthropology for Christian Workers*, Techny, Divine Word Publications, 1963 ; also by the journals *Practical Anthropology* and *Anthropological Quarterly*.

supposedly a strictly objective and scientific description. Today anthropology has to justify its existence by application to the felt needs of man. It is called out of its "ivory towers" of "science for science's sake" to be responsible for society. This notion was developed recently by Gjessing in an article "The Social Responsibility of the Social Scientist".[3] With this reorientation it seems appropriate that some anthropological comment be made on the theme of the Bangkok conference.

Furthermore the region between mission studies and anthropology, long a kind of no-man's-land, can no longer be so regarded. A new type of missionary case study has appeared, with either an anthropological section or anthropological themes running through it. These studies speak to wider circles than the particular countries they research.[4] They show, what Luzbetak has articulated, that "the most basic human problem in missionary work" is "the socio-cultural context" and thus anthropology is "an essential aspect of missionary formation — not a 'side-branch' ".[5]

This article explores some anthropological dimensions of culture change, culture and identity, and salvation in this new era of Christian mission. In the study of man's "consciousness of man" (identity) the anthropologist, because of his cross-cultural explorations, has been called "intensified man".[6] His theory requires a data base of tested and measured information from precisely defined localities, groups of people or themes. Techniques vary, but good theory must be built on case studies.

The same is good for missiology. Publications like the CWME World Studies of Churches in Mission and the Church Growth Series coming from Fuller Theological Seminary, California, are serious attempts at developing missiological theory on a basis of field research. Without this theory/research "marriage" accomplishments and failures of the

[3] GJESSING, GUTORM, "The Social Responsibility of the Social Scientist", *Current Anthropology*, 9, 5, 397-403, 1968.
[4] LALIVE D'EPINAY, CHRISTIAN, *Haven of the Masses : A Study of the Pentecostal Movement in Chile*, London, Lutterworth Press, 1969 ; TAYLOR, JOHN V. and LEHMANN, DOROTHEA, *Christians of the Copper Belt : The Growth of the Church in Northern Rhodesia*, London, SCM Press, 1961 ; and TIPPETT, A. R., *Solomon Islands Christianity : A Study in Growth and Obstruction*, London, Lutterworth Press, 1967, are examples of this kind of missiology.
[5] *Op. cit.*, pp. 18-19.
[6] KING, ARDEN R., "The Old Ethnography : The Consciousness of Man", in *Concepts and Assumptions in Contemporary Anthropology*, Athens, Southern Anthropology Society, Univ. of Georgia Press, 1969.

churches could not be fully shared. Although each situation is unique, nevertheless there are consistencies and continuities which need to be understood if we are to be efficient in our stewardship under God.

We ought to be, Janus-like, looking both backwards and forwards. Mission, like culture, has a past, present and future. The operational dynamics and opportunities of today must take cognizance of the collective experiences of yesterday and keep an eye on the goals of tomorrow. We reject the lessons of the past to our peril. We look forward into an unknown future, the contours of which are beginning to form. Some braver souls, like David Barrett,[7] dare to project what may be expected. Barrett sees a strong black Christianity with African values by the year 2000. Against this we set sociological predictions without number, foretelling the demise of Christianity by that date. For most people the only certainty is "today". Here we stand at a point of time, trying to be aware of its dangers and alert to its opportunities. We would eliminate the errors of the past but preserve its abiding values. On the other hand we must articulate programmes for tomorrow that are credible and realistic. Something has to be terminated ; but something has to be transmitted forward. Today is a *synapse*. Impulses of energy generated yesterday have to pass on into the systems of tomorrow. At this point of space and time, and from this mental set, we consider salvation, and culture and identity. To sharpen the issues I shall arrange them as a series of conceptual dyads.

The danger of conflict in debates in the theory of both anthropology and mission is semantic. Nothing holds up progress (i.e. the application of adequate theory to real life needs and situations) like disputations over semantics. We strive for a statement to which all may subscribe, knowing full well that when we come to act on it we will interpret it differently. I hope these dyads will point up the confluence of issues of possible misunderstanding and encounter. They are fundamental distinctions that need to be recognized before Christian mission can set forth its goals clearly, or discover adequate methodologies for presenting Salvation Today and understanding Cultural Identity.

---

[7] BARRETT, DAVID, "Are your missions big enough ?" *Church Growth Bulletin*, V, 5, 362-366, 1969. "A.D. 2000 : 350 Million Christians in Africa", *International Review of Mission*, X, No. 233, 39-54, 1970.

Change and Continuity

No aspect of anthropology has claimed more attention since the war than culture change. More and more the agents of change (including medical, educational and agricultural workers, missionaries and traders) are receiving advice from applied anthropologists.[8] Before the war "primitive" societies were studied frantically lest their cultures should disappear. Anthropologists protected them and told missionaries to go home. Cultural relativism was common talk. True there is something about cultural relativism which every anthropologist and missionary has to learn — namely, that every society has its own patterns, values, world view, and right to make its own decisions and to do things in its own way. But it is just as bad to "cage" a community and treat a people as guinea-pigs for experiment or museum display as to inflict paternalistic, western, ecclesiastical systems upon them. The survival anthropologists were, in their own way, just as ethnocentric and paternalistic as any missionary. The cross-cultural agent of change must tread the road to cultural relativism (if only to understand), but he must not bog down there.[9] This would leave him with a static view of society that just is not true. Important research today is considering the cultural significance of man as human. This does not ignore the relativity of cultural groups in this pluralistic world (indeed early relativists like Herskovits and Linton [10] also searched for universals in human societies), but recognizes that these diverse homogeneous groups have to live in close proximity and to interact. To cut off tribes by isolation for survival sake is to condemn them to stagnation and extinction. But the more they interact the more they change.

Anthropology speaks to Christian mission about the nature of change. First, change is going on all the time. The notion that tribal societies

[8] For example, ARNSBERG, CONRAD M. and NIEHOFF, A. H., *Introducing Culture Change : A Manual for Americans Overseas ?*, Chicago, Aldine Publishing Co., 1964 ; SPICER, ED. H. (ed.), *Human Problems in Technological Change*, New York, John Willey Sons, 1952 ; BARNETT, HOMER G., *Anthropology and Administration*, Evanston, Row, Peterson Co., 1956 ; MEAD, MARGARET, *Cultural Patterns and Technological Change*, New York, The New American Library, 1955 ; FOSTER, GEORGE M., *Traditional Cultures and the Impact of Technological Change*, New York, Harper and Row, 1962 ; *Applied Anthropology*, Boston, Little, Brown and Co., 1969 ; LINTON, RALPH (ed.), *Science of Man in the World Crisis*, New York, Columbia Univ. Press, 1945 ; BUNKER, ROBERT and ADAIR, JOHN, *The First Look at Strangers*, New Brunswick, N.J., Rutgers Univ. Press, 1959, to mention only a few.

[9] GOLDSCHMIDT, WALTER, *Comparative Functionalism : An Essay in Anthropological Theory*, Berkeley, University of California Press, 1966.

[10] HERSKOVITS, MELVILLE J., *Man and His Works : The Science of Cultural Anthropology*, New York, Alfred A. Knopf, 1951 ; LINTON, RALPH, *The Study of Man*, New York, 1936.

are static is a myth. There always has been change, however slight. The speed varies, but this is nothing new. Change is not necessarily bad. It indicates when a society is ready for it. Every society has inbuilt mechanisms for effecting change. The cross-cultural agent of change needs to be aware of them and operate through these indigenous institutions, procedures and persons.

Second, any changes advocated by the agent of change, have to be seen, not as foreign impositions, but as options advocated, which will be accepted or rejected by the target group. The community will have its own pattern for decision-making. Except where Christianization has come with military conquest, Christian missions were advocated and accepted, not imposed. If the Protestant missionaries were to blame for the Western form of their advocacy of the Gospel, their fault was the same as that of every salesman and TV commercial — namely, they presented only one option. Their convictions were ethnocentrically Western. Often they failed to see that Christian worship, and indeed the Gospel itself, could have "indigenous garments". (I generalize. Some early missionaries were good anthropologists.) They tended to oversimplify the option as a "package deal" : the old way or the new, the darkness or the light. However, for whatever motivation, the people made the choice.

In the new era of mission two things should be kept in mind. First, the option of an indigenous theology and form of worship must always be presented. The target people must never be confronted with a foreign ecclesiology and theology as the only option to their old way. Second, and quite apart from this, Christianity is not the only foreign option today. Millions in Africa, New Guinea and Indonesia, for instance, have discovered that their old religious system is no longer adequate for the new day, and have reached the psychological and cultural moment for change, as described by Kroeber [11] and Barnett [12]. Innovate they certainly will, but Christianity is competing with Islam, Secularism, Communism and maybe Neopagan Syncretism. The basic difference between the old and new eras of mission is the current multi-option. In the light of this, conversions may have a better motivation in the new

---

[11] KROEBER, A. L., *Anthropology*, New York, Harcourt, Brace & Co, 1948.
[12] BARNETT, HOMER C., *Innovation : The Basis of Cultural Change*, New York, McGraw-Hill Book Co., 1953 ; *Anthropology and Administration*, Evanston, Row, Paterson & Co., 1956.

era. Some anthropologists have pressed that agents of change should deliberately confront peoples considering change with all the options, and also discuss the compatibility of possible options with their own way of life.[13] By the same token, this demands the presence of a Christian advocate in every dynamic situation, as I think the scriptural commission obligates the Church anyway. I see only two valid reasons for withdrawing missionaries : (1) if they are foreigners and a strong local witness has already been established, and (2) because of repeated rejection (Luke 10 : 10 ff.).

Third, culture change does not have to be chaotic or violent. Violence and revolution may remove certain obstructions, but they always leave scars on the society. Some priceless values are inevitably lost. Many effective cultural and social changes have been won by less destructive methods : literature, music, drama, recreation, revival, to mention a few. The battle against slavery in England was fought in pulpit and parliament, as were also the labour reforms after the industrial revolution.

Over against culture change stand the essential cultural continuities. When societies change slowly these continuities stand out as stabilizers which permit change without serious dislocation. They relate in particular to the moral fibre. A society which loses these is in a bad way. For example, a fundamental unit of social stability is the family. When the family falls apart, a whole complex of personal relationships, enculturative education, inter-dependence, security and responsibility is dismembered with it. This is so whether the family is monogamous or polygamous, nuclear or extended. It is reinforced by rites of passage, the value system and religion. The family, then, is one of these continuities. The value system itself is another, and so is religion. When any of these breaks down, the society passes into a state of severe stress. A functional substitute may be found for the broken institution : but a society without a value system or religion (communism is a religion, or faith-system, at the negative pole) or a family pattern is heading for anarchy and extinction.

The Christian missionary enterprise has operated under many changing forms, but its essential continuity, its value base, down through history has been the Bible, where the commission to bring salvation to the nations

---

[13] FOSTER, GEORGE M., *Traditional Cultures and the Impact of Technological Change*, New York, Harper & Row, 1962 ; *Applied Anthropology*, Boston, Little, Brown & Co., 1969.

is set forth. As long as this is regarded as the revelation of God it survives as a continuity through changing techniques of mission and changing situations in which mission operates. But if the notion of the Bible as the revealed word of God to "man in mission" be allowed to disintegrate, we have merely a cultural artifact from ancient times, a museum piece, with no relevances beyond that of "any one's opinion".

"Development", "humanization" and "liberation" are politico-ethical terms. If we desire to use them theologically, then we presuppose that the notion of the Bible as the revelation of God in mission is one of the continuities, which must be preserved through change in the new era of mission, and the terms acquire an evangelical meaning. Thus the attitude to the Bible is crucial. Unless we agree that it provides the criteria for mission, and place it in the continuity rather than the change category, there is little hope for agreement about the nature of Salvation Today.

Destruction and Construction

Margaret Mead's question arises from the current process of cultural change. It raises ethical and theological problems because it affects the human situation and man's survival. Forty years ago Alexis Carrel [14] pointed out that mankind was heading for trouble because the various branches of intellectual endeavour were not progressing at the same rate. He doubted man's spiritual capacity to control responsibly the new knowledge he was acquiring. The daily news, the war reports, the existence of terrifying bombs remind us that we live in a dramatically dynamic world with "terrible powers of destruction" set over against "limitless powers of construction" — all in the hands of men. Margaret Mead told this to the American Association for the Advancement of Science sixteen years ago. She saw in this "capacity of man to destroy or construct" a sore need for vision, a realization that the world was unsafe, a need to understand the magnitude of this power and to use it responsibly.

About the same time Charles Coulson addressed the World Methodist Conference on "Nuclear Power and Christian Responsibility". [15] He

---

[14] CARREL, ALEXIS, *Man the Unknown*, New York, Harper and Bros., 1935.
[15] COULSON, CHARLES, "Nuclear Power and Christian Responsibility", *Proc. World Methodist Conference*, Lake Junaluska, 1956.

concluded with a dramatic illustration of this dichotomy — a single man with his hand on a single lever to push or to pull, to launch an atomic weapon on the Atlantic coast or to light an inland city with atomic power. He asked if scientific man, who now had in his hands the powers of God, had yet learned enough of the mind of God to use them responsibly. After the sixties we agree with Mead that man needs vision of meaning and responsibility.

In the face of man's inhumanity to man, of fear in all its forms, the threat of destruction, the possibility of another world war from which no victor could emerge, certainly there is need for salvation in social terms — quite apart from the traditional meaning. This is ethical in that it deals with human relationships. "The unity of man" wrote Wolf,[16] "is a process of the involvement of man with man, through the medium of human culture". Theoretically this kind of salvation should merely require man living with his kind in peace and achieving Mead's "vision of meaning and responsibility". *Secular* anthropology can go no further than that — and that is only theoretically possible, however worthy a goal. The problem, of course, is human nature, man's proneness to sin and his stubborn refusal to love his neighbour as himself.

The point McGavran [17] keeps raising is that you must get man right with God before you can get him right with his fellow man. You can go so far with dialogue and constitutional procedures, but as Colin Morris recently reacted to an appealing address on the relief of poverty, in the final analysis the inequities behind poverty spring from human sin. Ultimately it is a theological issue. Then, as believers who have come to terms with God and draw from His resources, redeemed man must look again on the human condition. "Vision of meaning and responsibility" now has new significance, not as a hope or wish, but as stewardship under God. Then we must certainly play our part in the "saving" of society, first by resisting its injustices and then by appropriating its constructive opportunities. This is *Christian*, not secular anthropology. The articulation hangs together because the culmination of a science of man is the "new man in Christ".

[16] WOLF, ERIC R., *Anthropology*, Englewood Cliffs, Prentice-Hall Inc., 1964.
[17] McGAVRAN, D. A., *The Church in a Revolutionary Age*, St. Louis, Christian Board of Publications (Multigraphed), 1955.

Restatement and Reformulation

I have discussed the creative tension between change and continuity. The inherent capacity of society for change is itself a continuity. What has been said of cultural values applies also to both anthropological and missiological theory. New theoretical dimensions are continually being explored, but they spring from existing theory. The great anthropological theorists — Tylor, Codrington, Frazer, Boas, Malinowski — have all had later anthropologists modify their theory. Yet their basic discoveries have been restated from time to time.

Tylor's possession theory [18] was a valid frame of reference for researching the phenomenon, but he tied it to unilinear evolution and the phase of savagery, a notion subsequently discarded. The theory had to be restated without erroneous presuppositions. The part which stood the test of time is still used for possession studies.

Likewise, Malinowski's concept of a new autonomous entity [19] was put forward within the colonial situation, which he believed to be the "given" within which it was to work. Colonialism broke down but there is still vital truth in the concept, which calls for restatement for post-colonial situations. Malinowski resisted the dualism of culture clash, the weaker perishing before the dominant. He saw the new autonomous entity (identity) with administrator, missionary, trader, farmer and chief interacting and inter-relating. A restatement of this principle currently operates in some young nations where British planters, for example, have taken out local citizenship.

Restatement is significant also in missiological theory. Many Church Growth studies show how remarkable growth has been achieved by the restatement of some biblical principle for new conditions. Acts 13 has been adapted as a model for many church-planting missions, and Acts 6 for organic church growth by role-creation. The Great Commission has been repeatedly restated for new situations through history ; Brancati, Carey, John Williams all did so, with significant effect.

Over against these restatements of theory, and distinguished from them, have been radical reformulations of missionary procedures and tech-

---

[18] TYLOR, E. B., *Primitive Culture*, London, John Murray, vol. 2, 1891.
[19] MALINOWSKI, BRONISLAW, "The Anthropology of Changing African Cultures", editorial introductory essay in *Methods of Study of Culture Contact in Africa*, London, International African Institute (OUP), 1938.

niques, which the new situations demand. Thus Carey's *Enquiry* [20] brings out clearly how he was concerned with the world changes of his times : the discoveries of the great navigators, new navigational techniques, newly discovered tribes and languages ; and how he himself became involved in a mission beyond the technology of the apostles. He saw what was wrong with the Church of his day, with abundant resources and no outreach, and corrected this by methodological reformulations. The restatement of the Great Commission for the new era was one thing. Reformulation of methods and policies to act upon it was another. They are found side by side in his *Enquiry*. One reason why the Uppsala drafts drew fire from the Conservatives was that reformulations were there in abundance, but the restatements were omitted. It is axiomatic that any reformulation of missionary technique should begin with a restatement of the Great Commission.

Unity and Uniformity

The planners of the Bangkok consultation have wisely provided for one section to deal with Culture and Identity. One must admit that our progress in understanding the identity of minority groups, ethnic or social, has been either slow or unrealistic. The Western world has a questionable notion of the rightness of majority rule. The wrongness of minority rule that is despotic and oppressive is apparent, but at the opposite pole is something which can become just as destructive. Anthropological case studies have frequently shown that social and ethnic groups, caught in the networks of a large nation, frequently have to forfeit their cultural identity or face possible extinction.

When I visit an Indian reservation I find that people want to retain their cultural identity, to follow their traditional way of life, to preserve their values and skills, and speak their own language. But there is no real hope for survival as such, no economic future unless they accept the values and language of the "main culture". They hear the country saying, "Retain your cultural identity and die, or adapt and compete with us, for you belong to the nation, and the main culture is the national culture". Either minority or majority rule can become inconsiderate and despotic.

---

[20] CAREY, WILLIAM, *An Enquiry into the Obligations of Christians to use means for the Conversion of the Heathens*, London, Hodder & Stoughton (1892 Facsimile), 1792.

The same situation exists in bi-cultural or multi-cultural communities or congregations. A Spanish-American pastor in Los Angeles has English and Spanish speaking members in his congregation and possibly other groups. If any group is neglected, it will probably be a minority one. But without the opportunity for participation in the on-going programme they lose identity. There is no belongingness.

Integration and assimilation have been presented as "salvation". Sermons by the hundred have been preached on "being one in Christ" and on there being "neither Jew nor Gentile". We all understand that somehow we must learn to live together ; but we advocate it in two very different ways. I believe the notion of Unity or Uniformity exposes the problem.

Before men can live happily together they have to see themselves biologically as the same : human beings. Anthropology has long been saying that our ideas about race are a tragic myth. A good, short statement on this is Kluckhohn's chapter on it in his book, *Mirror for Man*.[21] On the other hand we make a bad mistake when we confuse race and culture. Every man, anthropologically speaking, has two identities — one as a member of the human race (which means theologically, that he is one for whom Christ died) and the other as a member of some specific culture, from which he derives his habits, his language and his outlook on life. A pastor or missionary may be well aware of human identity, but tragically oblivious to cultural identity. The former concerns the right of every man to hear the Gospel and to have the option of accepting or rejecting it. The latter determines the languages and manner in which it should be communicated, and also the patterns in which his new life in Christ is nurtured and exercised. If we decline to offer the "gospel in mission" we deny man his true human identity. If we offer it in culturally unacceptable forms we reject the cultural identity.

In theological debates this often surfaces as the Unity-Uniformity issue. Uniformity presupposes a "melting-pot" and claims integration on a basis of human identity. Unity operates on a biological model, like the scriptural Body of Christ, with differing parts functioning in inter-relationship, doing his saving work in the world ; or alternatively as many folds whose sheep belong to one flock under one Shepherd. I cannot find the concept of uniformity in the Scriptures. Moreover the validity

[21] KLUCKHOHN, CLYDE, *Mirror for Man : A Survey of Human Behavior & Social Attitudes*, Greenwich, Conn., Fawcett Publications, 1957.

of the "melting-pot idea" in the megalopolis has been heavily attacked by critics. The reader might read the book *Beyond the Melting Pot*.[22] Scripture and anthropology seem to be in step in recognizing the importance of diversity in unity ; which suggests that the true meaning of integration is discovering how blacks and whites, Europeans and Africans, can live and work together without giving up their cultural identities.

If we state salvation in terms of sociology (instead of eschatologically), as the preliminary papers of Bangkok seem to ask, it would seem to me that such social salvation should stimulate some experience wherein men of various cultures would come to respect each other's ways of life, share dialogue in love, bear mutual burdens and manifest different gifts without the sacrifice of identity. However, this cannot be accomplished on any common base from the social sciences. I can only see it as a possibility when the parties concerned become new men in Christ : but that is a Christian and not a secular anthropology. Then, as parts of the Body of Christ, they would need to retain their distinctiveness, their cultural gifts and identity.

Missionaries who have succeeded in escaping from the house on the hill-top, have itinerated frequently, learned to eat the food, speak the language, sleep in the leaf house, and cultivated deep friendships across cultures, have invariably found a deepening of their own Christian theology because of the rapport. I believe we will never appreciate the wholeness of Christian theology until "the nations" have added their contributions to it.[23] My Fijian brethren taught me to love the Old Testament. Diversity in loving unity brings this, not living in uniformity.

This is a post-conversion experience. I am not speaking of dialogue with men of other faiths, but with Christian men of other cultures. We still have much of the "working out of our salvation" to discover, and having discovered it, I am sure we will witness better to men of other faiths. I recall how the poetry of the Indian Christian, Tilak, came through to me with the startling discovery that there was far more

---

[22] GLAZER, N. & MOYNIHAN, D. P., *Beyond the Melting Pot*, Cambridge, Mass., MIT Press, 1963.

[23] All the Americas, for example, have yet to learn from the Negro who "does not come empty-handed seeking equality ; he possesses values that need to be added to American culture(s)". MITCHELL, HOWARD E., "The Urban Crisis and Search for Identity", *Social Casework*, 50, 1, 10-15, 1969.

in the theology of sacrifice than I had dreamed. Tilak retained his cultural identity in his poetry, and my life would have been poorer and less dedicated had this not come my way. When we recognize cultural diversity we begin to draw from it.

Liberation and Reconciliation

A large part of the world is in a violent mood today, and this is reflected in revolution and the theology of liberation. This is an interesting anthropological phenomenon. The theology itself has a biblical undergirding and the cry for liberation is a just cause. I believe the doctrine can be stated evangelically ; but, on the other hand, it is often politically manipulated with political goals. A Marxist interpretation is prominent among its many uses. Nevertheless, it is a salvation motif, and in Christian terms has something worth saying. The idea of liberation for individual and community is a valid goal.

On the other hand, a purely sociological liberation, in spite of physical improvement attained by the effort, is no guarantee for a liberated spirit. Without this liberation of spirit the "alienated", "truncated man", who by liberation is supposedly "integrated and made whole" is, in point of fact, neither integrated nor whole.

A graduate defending his thesis last week narrated his experiences with Latin American informants, who reacted against the word "reconciliation". Reconciliation mechanisms are not peculiarly Christian. They are widespread across the world in non-Western societies. The informants' rejection of the term was due to their feeling that reconciliation was a passive procedure, an act of resignation, or at best a compromise. They could not conceptualize salvation in this term and talked of liberation, which suited better their feelings of aggression.

Now, reconciliation is by no means passive. It is an active thrust against the existence of social discord and often takes much courage to initiate. From a remote island in the Solomons to the hunting forest-dwellers of Southern Ethiopia I have seen non-Christian reconciliation mechanisms in operation — religious acts in the name of some deity, positive and premeditated. They differ from liberation by being corrective procedures within a social structure. Liberation is a destructive procedure of cultural change, setting people free from some form of oppression.

Anthropologically, reconciliation and liberation are opposites — one restoring society, the other resisting it. Yet both are forms of social salvation.

Interestingly enough both can be used as analogies for the work of Christ — as Reconciler and Liberator. In each case the earthly prototype is tentative, only effective within limitations, and confined to the here and now. In Christian terms reconciliation and liberation are results or outcomes of men meeting the Reconciler or Liberator face to face. Two questions arise for consideration : (1) Is a purely sociological liberation or reconciliation adequate ? (2) To what extent is man so recreated in Christ that he becomes himself a liberator and reconciler in the community where God has placed him ? Once again, secular anthropology takes us only so far. Are we to stop there, with the ultimate limited by man's own capacity ? Christian anthropology is a better *finale*. In Christ, the perfect Man, man transcends the limitations of his natural capacities, and as a new man in Christ he finds a new dimension for his selfhood.

Conclusions

I have been pressing throughout that in an age of rapid cultural change, like the present, dramatic discontinuities are inevitable. Frequently they are absolutely essential. They do not necessarily have to lead to chaos. They are often opportunities for new beginnings after failure. Nevertheless, these discontinuities (sometimes conceptual, more often perhaps methodological, technical or practical) must be held in a state of reasonable equilibrium by certain continuities (more often conceptual). Some things survive. Certain principles and laws (as also in business, economics or science) have to be restated repeatedly. Machines, operations, techniques and patterns may change, but principles go on, at least until better substitutes are found. If mission is to remain Christian, certain ideas must be recognized as basic. People must go on believing them. When context and environment change, new communicative approaches must be found for the very reason that fundamentals still have to be transmitted.

Discontinuities, revolutions, new beginnings and new eras are never quite absolute, however drastic. Much literature supporting such discontinuities fails to recognize the essential continuities — and I do not exclude writing on Salvation Today. If the participants at the Bangkok Conference are to achieve their stated purpose of understanding salvation in terms of contemporary experience, the danger is that, being enthused over necessary innovations and programmes, they may fail to relate them to our Lord's idea of mission itself.

A sad commentary on our unwillingness to be realistic is that three decades after a plea for "a typology of minority groups" [24] to identify problems of minority-dominant group relations, and hundreds of anthropological monographs on our pluralistic societies, our preaching should still be bogged down, trying to enforce main-culture uniformity. A systematic survey by a research team is still required. Where cultural pluralism exists it must be recognized. Unrecognized, ignored or suppressed and the whole community (world on the largest panorama) is under stress ; but recognized and allowed for, it may become a positive value. Roger Keesing called it "a crucial human resource", and went on :

> The cancelling out of cultural differences and the emergence of a standardized world culture might — while solving some problems of political integration — deprive men of sources of wisdom and vision, and a reservoir of diversity and alternatives, he cannot afford to lose. [25]

Any study of Salvation Today must recognize (1) the character of the human situation, within which we are to engage in mission, so that the thrust of the operation may be culturally, relevantly and appropriately equipped for effective engagement with the real issues ; and (2) the character of the human condition and the abiding theological principles which speak to it, without which the effort can be no more than a benevolent humanitarianism, not necessarily Christian at all ; and which would lead to an age of "mission" even more exposed to paternalism and ethnocentricity than that from which we are emerging.

As a missionary anthropologist I see the basic components of a currently valid missiological theory as anthropological and theological, [26] the former

[24] In 1944 Wirth proposed the criteria for such measurement : (1) Identification of number, size and location ; (2) degree of friction and amount of exclusion or participation ; (3) nature of social arrangements governing relationships, and (4) possible goals for both groups. Cf. WIRTH, LOUIS, "The Problem of Minority Groups" in Linton's *Science of Man in the World Crisis*, New York, Columbia Univ. Press, 1945.

[25] KEESING, ROGER M. and FELIX, M., *New Perspectives in Cultural Anthropology*, New York, Holt, Rinehart & Winston.

[26] TIPPETT, A. R., "The Components of Missionary Theory", *Church Growth Bulletin*, VI, 1-3, 1969.

speaking to the human situation and the latter to the human condition. Our Lord clearly indicated to his disciples an approaching ministry *in the world* and *to the world* (John 17 : 18) ; yet men were to be brought to him as the only way to the Father (14 : 6). After his departure the subsequent record indicates that they both restated and acted upon this directive. In those days of shock following the crucifixion, the risen Lord reinforced their confidence by pointing out two basic continuities — the written and living Word (Luke 24 : 25-27, 30-32).

PART II

Reports Of The Consultation

4

SALVATION TODAY: A CRITICAL REPORT

Manuel J. Gaxiola

A world-wide meeting to discuss the theme, SALVATION TODAY, convened in the outskirts of the city of Bangkok, Thailand, December 29, 1972- January 12, 1973, under the auspices of the Commission on World Mission and Evangelism of the World Council of Churches. According to Leon Howell, there were 325 persons present, including 16 Roman Catholics, 27 women and 16 youth. 70 came from Europe, 56 from Asia, 30 from North America, 22 from Africa, 16 from Latin America, 7 from the Pacific, 6 from the Middle East and 5 from the Caribbean. Howell also informs us that

> CWME emerged when the International Missionary Council (IMC) integrated with the WCC at the New Delhi Assembly in 1961. This is the CWME's Third Assembly ... The WCC, based in Geneva, Switzerland, is composed of 26 Protestant, Anglican, Orthodox and Old Catholic Churches and councils in 90 countries.

The meeting was divided into two parts. The first part of the meeting (December 29-January 8) was devoted to the study of SALVATION TODAY, and the second part (January 9-12) was devoted to the Third Assembly of the Commission on World Mission and Evangelism (CWME). The writer attended only the first part of the meeting.

There were several Bible study groups, groups for meditation, groups using music and the Arts, and groups on health and healing. The whole group was also divided into sections:

Section I - Culture and Identity
  A. Dialogue with People of Living Faiths
  B. Christian Identity and Racial Identity
  C. Cultural Change and Conversion
Section II - Salvation and Social Justice
  A. In a World of Violent Revolutionary Change
  B. In Situations of Economic Exploitation

    C. In Relation to National Planning
    D. In Relation to Local Struggles
  Section III - Churches Renewed in Mission
    A. Churches in Relationship
    B. Growing Churches and Renewal
    C. The Local Mission of Each Church

The writer was assigned to one group on Meditation, but for
reasons that will be easy to understand after further reading,
he decided to change to a Bible Study group that was composed of about 15 persons. The writer was also a member of
Sub-section C (Cultural Change and Conversion) in which there
were about 30 people, and was privileged to present an action
report on Protestantism in Mexico. Drawing from his experience in sociology and research, the writer was able to explain how, in the Mexican experience, cultural change is an
agent for conversion and at the same time conversion is an
agent for cultural change. The only other action report in
this group was presented by a lady minister from the Broadway
Presbyterian Church in New York and who works among the Jesus
People in that area.

The Bible study groups were rightly praised as perhaps
the most meaningful and useful of all the meetings, the reason
being, first, that the groups were rather small and there was
ample opportunity for everybody to participate and, second,
the message of the Bible, and not what each one thought nor
the particular teachings of a Church or school, was given special preeminence in each Bible study group, and in most cases
there was a remarkable affinity of thought. Some groups found
special joy in their shared study of the Scriptures and this
joy was made evident in the reflecting meetings and also in
written statements. This was particularly true in Bible Study
No. 3, where Dr. Arthur F. Glasser was the Reflector (See The
Conference Journal, Nos. 6/7 for Jan. 5/6).

We cannot, however, deny that there were in each and every
group a few people who clearly sought to get across what appears
to be the main preoccupation of the WCC, and which to the eyes
of many Evangelicals does not represent a genuine concern for
the fulfilling of the Great Commission as traditionally understood, but rather pretends to involve the Church in social,
political and economical concerns which cannot be but secondary.
As one delegate said in a plenary meeting, "We have devoted
more time to the discussion of the social and political implications of the gospel but not to the gospel." Many people felt
that the resolutions to be taken after many of the participants
had left, were actually "prefabricated" and would in no way
reflect the biblical insights that had been gained in the Bible

study groups. Others felt that the breaking of the conference
into small groups was an attempt at "manipulation" in the sense
that the real issues would not be discussed at the level where
it really mattered, which was at the level of the whole conference. The comments by Dr. Peter Beyerhaus in this respect
(The Conference Journal, No. 4, Jan. 3, page 5) seem very
pertinent:

> The announcement of the Bangkok theme, "Salva-
> tion Today" raised the hope in us that this
> would be an excellent opportunity to discuss
> these central biblical concerns on a highly
> representative level. But the structure of
> this conference, its division into small cells
> which are not expected to produce statements or
> reports has again made it impossible to come to
> terms on this issue.

It is only fair to add that as far as we could determine,
in every meeting, both in the small groups and in the plenaries and also in written comments, there was freedom of speech
and everybody was heard politely by the others.

PRELIMINARIES

Under this heading include all the activities that took
place from Friday, December 29 through Sunday, December 31.

The opening ceremony on Friday at 4:30 P.M. was a little
of a disappointment to this observer for no prayer was offered
to God our Father and it is hard to believe it was an over-
sight. Her Royal Highness Princess Poon Pismai Diskul, member
of the ruling family of Thailand and President of the World
Fellowship of Buddhists, was to give a speech of welcome, but
in her absence it was read by Aiem Sangkhavasi, General Secretary of the same fellowship. What was said in the speech
might please some of those who were present, but to others it
was rather disturbing, especially in the following parts (Conference Journal, No. 2, Jan. 1):

> All genuine religious people, despite the differ-
> ence of outward trappings, know that they are
> heading towards the same destination, the differ-
> ence being that each has chosen the path he pre-
> fers. In this respect the Buddha once said,
> "Virtuous men understand each other".
>
> Besides belief and unbelief, like love and hate,
> respect and contempt, cannot be forced. Each
> depends on growth and tendency. It is because

of this fact that there are several remedies for
the diseased minds. This is to match the growth
and tendency of an individual and also the kind
of disease he is suffering from. But all spiritual remedies, be they called Buddhism, Christianity and others, produce the same effect for
those who take them: recovery from disease and
the consequent health, vigour and a Greater Life.
Whether this be called Nibbana or Union with God
or an Eternal Life does not matter.

A delegate from Germany (Conference Journal, No. 3,
Jan. 2) reacted to this speech in the following manner:

If Buddhists are the same good human beings as
we are, then they do not need mission any more.
Of course, they do not have the Gospel, but they
have other precious books.

Thus from the very beginning there was an excellent opportunity for a real and thorough debate on the meaning of
SALVATION TODAY, for it was easy to see clearly what the real
issue (as explained later) was, but unfortunately the opportunity was missed.

The Church of Christ in Thailand, which is the only church
of any size in that country (and is ecumenically related) also
presented a program of welcome, including a message by Rev.
Wichean Watakeecharoen, General Secretary. When we remember
that in Thailand there is only one Christian for every 1400
people, we must not be surprised if all the Churches in that
country, including those associated with the WCC, strive for
growth in membership, but when this concern was mentioned in
passing by the Reverend Watakeecharoen, it hurt the sensibil-
ities of some, as witnessed by the following statement (Conference Journal, No. 2, Jan. 1) by a delegate from Germany:

The sermon was very bad, representing the revivalistic theology of the Church of Christ in Thailand.
The enumeration of "so many souls saved" slaps the
whole dialogue in the face.

Dr. Thomas Wieser presented on December 30 a report on the
SALVATION TODAY study that was conducted in many parts of the
world previous to the Bangkok meeting. In these earlier studies you can already discern where the Conference was heading.
After mentioning what some Orthodox theologians had said about
salvation as a process from Creation to Redemption that includes both "heaven" and "earth", Dr. Wieser inserted a comment which could be taken as typical of ecumenical thinkers
(Report on the Study, page 5):

As we attempt to understand salvation in terms of
such a comprehensive process, we are, of course
not automatically eliminating the distinctions
mentioned previously. But we should at least be
freed from the pietistic concept of salvation as
primarily an affair between an individual and
God. In this connection a German report calls
for the "de-privatization" of salvation. Salvation Today cannot mean merely "individual application of a past event." Today we must seek
to "relate eschatological faith to the concrete
historical realities in a way that the societal
involvement of human experience becomes evident."

Referring to these issues and admitting they were the most
controversial, Dr. Wieser also said that the Bangkok meeting
was just "another setting in which to debate them" and then
mentioned the possibility that they could be recognized as
"false issues". The debate was actually "defused" (Dr.
Wieser's term) for the simple reason that there was no opportunity for such a debate, as the only "concrete" resolutions
had to deal with other matters. Although there were Evangelicals present who could perhaps have focused the debate on its
real biblical implications, their contribution was almost nil,
perhaps for the reason that they lacked coordination and did
not adopt the right strategy, and also because there was little hope that their viewpoint would be accepted by the majority. An unnamed correspondent for the *Theological News*, a
quarterly newsletter of the Theological Assistance Programme
of the World Evangelical Fellowship (Vol. 5, No. 1, Jan. 1973,
page 4) offers the following explanation:

It was predictable that divergent approaches would
be presented because there had been no serious
wrestling with the nature of salvation. The historical redemptive aspect was low-keyed and where
the feeble voice did emerge it was from orthodox
and liturgical churches.

The evangelical voice was not articulated to any
great extent, partly because of the way in which
the delegations were chosen, and partly because
of the feeling of isolation. Dr. Arthur Glasser
made some precise evangelical contributions as
an invited guest, but his attempts were effectively filtered out in official releases.

It is unfortunate that Dr. Peter Beyerhaus tried
to precipitate debate on his Frankfurt Declaration, rather than on certain issues within the

setting of the theme. He was silenced by the voices
of the Third World claiming that this was not a
forum to push "Western Theology." This unjusti-
fied naming him as from the west weakened his
incisive contributions when the conference moved
to the plenary sessions.

The report by Dr. Phillip Potter, the out-going Director
of the CWME and now General Secretary of the WCC, was heard
on December 31 and was supposed to deal with "Christ's Mission and Ours in Today's World." It dealt primarily with the
political and social changes that have taken place in the
whole world between 1963 and 1972. Perhaps Dr. Potter was
thinking of Dr. Donald A. McGavran when he included a reference to "the two billion or more who have never heard it
(the gospel) in the lands which have lived for millenia by
other faiths," but the main thrust of the report was thoroughly secular and is perfectly in line with his idea, expressed in the same report, that "secularism, the process by
which man controls and is not enslaved by nature, is *thoroughly
biblical in its emphasis*" (italics mine). Beyerhaus (1971:
20, 21) had very aptly described what has happened before and
he could very well have spoken about the Bangkok meeting when
he said:

> A final crucial undermining of the traditional
> understanding of mission is the recent, radical
> supplanting of all basic religious issues by
> political-social concerns. This movement per-
> meates all cultural spheres today and its in-
> fluence has been felt even in the Christian
> churches, particularly among young people.
> Fiedrich Gogarten, Ahrend van Leeuwen, Harvey
> Cox, and M.M. Thomas are connected with an in-
> fluential theological trend which interprets
> and justifies the secularization process as
> being a legitimate fruit of the Gospel.

What has been said up to now must be taken as general observations on the preliminaries of the Conference, the things
that took place from December 29 through January 31st. On
the first day of 1973 a new routine was begun with meetings
of groups and open hearings, and then came meetings of sections and plenary sessions until the end of the study part of
the Conference which came on the eighth of January. It is not
our intention to examine each detail of this part of the Conference; instead, we shall mention some specific issues and
facts which are of special interest to those who hold a more
conservative theological position.

SOME VERY GENUINE CONCERNS

This writer was fully impressed by two genuine concerns that were practically expressed during the Conference and which must be recognized for all their worth.

1) Obsolete Missionary Structures.

The missionary societies affiliated to the CWME seem to be ahead of some others in regard to this matter and they seem more willing than the others to turn the responsibility over to natives and in this way "indigenize" missions, while some more conservative missions seem to have as a policy the perpetuation of the foreign missionary as head of the operation, thus creating a situation of dependence which is harmful to the church in a native land. Since most of the missionaries in the past came from the more affluent, imperialistic nations, the missionary was seen, and in many cases, was, an agent for imperialism. The new day in which we are living requires a change of mentality and an end to missionary paternalism, the urgency being accelerated by the maturity of native leaders as evinced by many of the outstanding men who came especially from Asia and Africa. By contrast the Latin American ecumenicals seemed a little "sheepish."

However, the Asians and Africans who spoke about "change of missionary structures," "transfer of power," etc., seemed to hammer at the subject with more than ordinary vehemence, and this raised the question whether they were doing it out of a justified outrage against the methods of the early missionaries or whether it was a premeditated tactic aimed at gaining more concessions from the western missionary boards and societies--for this "transfer of power" includes, in the minds of many, the transfer of funds to native lands and the placing of all missionary personnel under the authority and control of the natives. This was one of the great mysteries of the Conference and a fact that was commented upon daily everywhere. When the author was given an opportunity to share his impressions of the meeting for the Conference Journal (No. 8, Jan 7, 1973, p.2), among other things he wrote:

> Latin Americans being neither white nor black nor
> yellow, but perhaps a pleasant chocolate-brown,
> look amazed at the "pummeling" the white Western
> brethren are taking from those who come in a
> different hue and who at every opportunity take
> the time (it is our time also) to tell us they
> are tired of Western teachings and customs that
> were imposed upon them, and to remind us how much

they have suffered the consequences from the mis-
guided missionary methods used in the past by whites,
whose intentions, values and methods are now resented and rejected by those who, in spite of all
past mistakes, are now Christians. Someone has called this a "sado-masochist duel" with one side hurl-
ing those recriminations and the other accepting
them *in toto* either by their silence on the floor
or by a grudging acceptance when talking in private
or in small groups. Although we do not condone the
mistakes and even abuses committed by missionaries
in the name of Jesus, we do think it is about time
some one stood up, be he white, black or yellow,
and say something nice about our Western brethren.
They need a pat on the back.

Leon Howell, the daily chronicler of the Conference, was
also very much aware of this situation and offered the following comments:

Blatant examples of the misuse of power, of which
all the delegates have a full supply, were discussed.
In the plenaries, in the sessions, in private discussions, this question came up in various forms.
And Third World delegates were puzzled by the absence of response, the silence of the Western delegates. Was it, in the words of Pauline Webb early
in the week, because those holding power understood
the "bankruptcy" of the Western culture and church
structures? Was it a sado-masochistic desire to
be purified by flagellation? Was it a tactic to
ride out the storm, a refusal to pour fuel on the
fire? One European church executive protested
his silence was not navel gazing. "I am honestly
listening for clues and would not want to say quickly
that my colleagues are not doing the same.

2) Service and Social Justice

It would be fair to say that the Churches affiliated with
the WCC have shown over and over a greater concern for the material condition of mankind and a greater desire to alleviate
as much as possible the human suffering which is due especially to congenital poverty or to the exploitation of man by
man. This, of course, stems out of a certain theological
understanding of mission and salvation which runs counterpoint
to that of most Evangelicals, but is nevertheless valid to the
point at which it does not invalidate the necessity for a personal experience of salvation. Most Evangelicals seem to be
more concerned with the restoration of man's vertical relationship, while non-evangelical ecumenicals are more preoccupied

with the horizontal relationship. We have no quarrel against
the declaration (Document #40, page 3) that "there is no economic justice without political freedom, no political freedom
without economic justice." We would criticize the involvement of the WCC in some struggles which are supposed to bring
greater social justice, especially in the cases in which the
WCC has been accused of providing funds for the purchase of
arms to be used by black guerrillas in Africa, but there are
other cases in which the WCC has been very active which de-
serve approval and applause from others. We could cite the
recent earthquake that destroyed part of the city of Managua,
Nicaragua and left thousands of people homeless and without
a job. The WCC through its Commission on Inter-Church Aid,
Refugee and World Service (CICARWS) was present in Managua
from the beginning and served through CEPAD (Comité Evangélico
Para Auxilio a Damnificados) as an "umbrella" for more than
twenty Churches that are providing relief for their own members and others, including the Apostolic Church of the Faith
in Christ Jesus (my own church), the United Pentecostal Church
and other conservative groups. The writer was able to verify,
during a recent trip to Managua, that CICARWS and other ecumenical relief groups have proven to be a blessing to that
city, providing food and shelter for many people of all faiths.

Beyerhaus (1971:58, 59) explains how "the hesitation of
evangelicals in past decades to be involved in social service
ought to be understood as a reaction to that contemporary tendency of the Church in which the call to a 'social gospel' went
hand in hand with a dangerously liberal undermining of the
Christian message," but then he explains how it was that
Evangelical Christianity has actually shown notable achieve-
ments in the field of social action which is now being overly
emphasized by the WCC. This point is taken in greater detail
by Orr (1965:219-229) who refers to "the abolition of the
slave trade, reform of prisons, emancipation of slaves, care
of the sick, education of the young, protection of worker and
the like" as accomplishments "by individuals nurtured in the
faith and worship of evangelical fellowship." In this respect,
Evangelicals would do well to heed to Beyerhaus' words (op.cit.):

> The present evangelical protest against ecumenical
> "horizontalism," because of its one-sidedness,
> is most certainly justified. But the answer to
> socio-ethical questions is not found by stubbornly
> ignoring them. This would result in a self-imposed
> isolationism which, to be sure, could not delay
> the great historical changes of our time, but which,
> by our lack of involvement, would expose us, when
> these changes prove to be catastrophic to humanity,
> to the judgment of God, the Lord of Mission.

DIALOGUE AND PROSELYTISM

A certain amount of dialogue was carried on at a practical
level during the Conference, first by the presence in the main
hall of a Thai "bhikku," or senior monk, a Thai intellectual
and a Ceylonese Buddhist United Nations officer, and, second,
by several visits which some of the delegates made to monas-
teries and Buddhist temples in the neighborhood. One came
away from the Conference with the impression that it is the
people from the WCC who are most interested in dialogue, while
to the others it does not seem a very urgent or needful matter.
In any case, we could not detect a positive affirmation of
Christian faith in these meetings nor a marked evangelistic
desire. We would then dispute Leon Howell's assertion that
"increasingly mission is being carried on in this spirit of
dialogue without the subsequent decrease in the sense of urgency in evangelism."

The writer had a brief and superficial experience that
made him see more poignantly the implications of an inter-
faith dialogue carried at the level which is favored by the
WCC and the accommodations that would have to be made by
Christians which might amount to compromise or perhaps even
to a capitulation of the faith. This happened at the group
that studied the Practice of Contemplation under the direction
of Father Murray Rogers, from Jerusalem. The writer considers
himself a mature and open-minded Christian, willing and able
to see the other man's side and to learn what others believe
and teach, in order to make an appropriate judgment, but after
one session at Father Rogers' group, he decided he would not
return the next day, for what was actually happening there,
in the writer's opinion, was not a presentation or explanation
of what others (Buddhists and the like) do and believe, but
rather a mixture of practices, Christian and non-Christian,
which could be classified as a syncretistic cult. A ceremony was conducted which was actually a Buddhist ceremony,
with all the parapharnelia that go with it and, of course,
with certain Christian elements which were relegated to second
place.

In particular, an Evangelical would object to two ideas
which were presented to the group and which could have very
serious implications in the future of the WCC. The first is
whether there is salvation for man outside Jesus Christ or
whether Acts 4:12 is still valid as our criteria for salvation. Father Rogers in his paper, "The Spirit: the milieu
of inter-faith dialogue," after criticizing fundamentalists
for condemning (according to him) "all others" and for hoping
that "outsiders" will some day tread "the true way to salvation," has this to say, which is typical of many who are engaged in this kind of dialogue:

Many of us are constrained to bear witness -
because of what has happened to us in our
own spiritual pilgrimage and in God's gifts
to us through those we grew up to think of as
"non-Christians" - to the realisation that
what happened to Peter and to his friends in
Cornelius' house in Caesarea has happened to
us also. Standing, as we believe, on Biblical
ground and oftentimes rejoicing while we trem-
ble, we joyfully accept the multiplicity of the
forms in which the Divine Spirit has used and
is using by which to bring men to the Father.
Did not Jesus Christ say that trees are recognized by their fruits? Who then can honestly
deny (unless he had not even approached the
tree?) the presence of the fruits of the Spirit
even in those who have never heard the Name of
Christ or who have never been incorporated into
his Mystical Body by baptism?

The second idea has to do with the place we assign to the
Hebrew and Greek Scriptures known to us as Old and New Testament or Holy Bible. Is the Bible our only rule of faith?
What is the place that we assign to the Scriptures of other
religions? Do we read them as simply a way to learn what
others consider Holy Writ or do we place them at the same
level as our own Bible. Father Rogers leaves no doubt as to
where he stands in this matter and we can honestly ask ourselves where all of this will lead in the future. In his
paper on "Upanishad Study", he tells the experience of a
"Bible study" group that has met in India and then he adds:

Such a prayerful study of the Upanishads by
Christian believers is surely warranted by
our own Scriptures both on the Old and New
Testaments. The texts mentioned below (among
others) point to the fact that the Spirit of
God has been working in the Gentiles all down
the ages, drawing them towards Christ and the
fulness (pleroma) of his presence in the Church
and in the world. From this we learn to expect that today also God is speaking to us
through the Gentiles' Scriptures, religious
traditions and spiritual experience, indeed,
all this is part of his call to us to be more
closely and deeply related to him in our life
as Christians.

The matter of proselytism was not officially brought before the Conference but it was easy to tell that this issue
was uppermost in the minds of some of the delegates. Although

we do not condone the practice of "sheep stealing", especially when it is based on slander (doctrinal or personal)
or in the use of material enticements for prospective converts (food, clothing, scholarships, even bribes), we do
believe that every church or preacher should be free to present his doctrine and practices to persons of other faith or
confession and everybody should be free to remain in the Church
in which he was born or to change to another of his choice.
To condemn proselytism per se or to curtail the freedom to
preach or to accept another doctrine on the pretext that the
people are already affiliated to a Church would be to ignore
that in every religion there are a majority of people who
are only nominal adherents of such a religion.

We find, for instance, that in Latin America the Catholic Church claims as Catholics close to 95% of all the people
for the simple reason that they were baptized in the Church
as infants, but it would be ridiculous for the same Church
to claim that all those people are practicing Catholics, much
less "born again" Christians. If the Protestant Churches
had thought so from the beginning and had accepted all those
Catholics as "fellow Christians," for the simple reason that
their name appeared in the baptismal records of the Roman
Catholic Church, there would hardly be a Protestant Church in
Latin America today and it is doubtful that those nominal
Catholics would be better off spiritually speaking if they
had stayed in their Church. Latin American Protestants justly
fear any move that hinders them from doing what they have been
doing so successfully for several generations even if many
bad things are said against proselytism.

It is a very significant fact that the only voices raised
against proselytism at the Conference came from the representatives of Churches in countries that have been traditionally
resistant to Protestant work but which to many Evangelicals
look very promising for the spreading of the gospel.

Reverend Hovhannes Aharonian, an Orthodox priest from
Lebanon, took to the floor of a plenary session to rant against
the missionaries who are coming to the Middle East to preach
the gospel and establish new churches, most of them, of course,
Protestant and possibly Evangelical. He said that there has
been a Christian Church (presumably the Syrian Orthodox Church
to which he belongs) for centuries, that all those people are
Christian and that it is a shame that others should come and
try to convert them. He asked for stern measures to make sure
that those missionaries will be prevented from continuing their
work.

Similar ideas and protests were aired by others during the Conference. It was most significant that one of the plenary sessions was chaired by Prof. G. Ammanuel Mikre-Selassie, delegate from the Ethiopian Orthodox Church, which is a full member of the WCC. According to *Newsweek* (January 15, 1973, page 50), Abuna Thewophlos, Patriarch of the Ethiopian Orthodox Church, is making good his threat "to exert all my energy against every teaching and movement that may battle against the Ethiopian Church." He has also "managed to enlist Emperor Haile Selassie's security apparatus in a campaign of terror against the 50,000 Ethiopians who have abandoned Orthodoxy and converted to the Full Gospel Church."

After describing how Pentecostals have been accused of treason and immorality, have been beaten and jailed and have had their Bibles burnt, *Newsweek* quotes one Pentecostal leader as saying: "The government has no evidence that we breed immorality. Unless, of course, you call it a sin to persuade Ethiopians that there is an alternative to the Orthodox Church."

"An alternative to the Orthodox Church." This is precisely what is now happening in those countries that have had for centuries a monopolistic or state religion, a monopoly that is beginning to be broken by Churches that preach a more aggressive gospel and expect a personal decision from every person who joins their ranks. Now we see some of these same old Churches joining the WCC and clamoring for a stop to the activities of other Churches within their own lands, and it will be interesting to find out what stand the WCC will take in this regard. The WCC accepts pluralism as a fact of life in the present world. Will those Churches, especially the Orthodox, accept denominational pluralism in their own back yard or will the WCC bow to their desire to retain their monopoly in religion by whatever means? To the writer this was one of the more pressing and foreboding questions raised at Bangkok.

THE IDEA OF MISSION

A man like the writer, born in a Church that grew from nothing to more than fifty thousand members and one thousand churches in half a century of active preaching, very naively would expect that a meeting of the Commission on World Mission and Evangelism would concern itself with the practical matters of establishing churches, sending missionaries, winning converts, etc., but, alas, mission is not understood in the same terms and evangelism, criticized for its "triumphalism," is seen as another form of "imperialism." This is very hard to understand to a poor Mexican from a Church that has even gone to other countries and has little or nothing to offer the people there except the promises of the

Bible, which in every case include "justice, peace and joy in-
spired by the Holy Spirit" (Romans 14:17). We see, then, that
our idea of mission is quite different from that of the CWME,
although in Bangkok we found among the delegates many who hold
an evangelical position and believe as Beyerhaus (1971:17)
does, that non-Christians are to be *converted*, new churches
to be *established*, and the name and plan of salvation of God
to be *glorified* (emphasis by the writer).

Granting that this difference of both opinion and goals
exists and wishing to learn what changes the future will bring,
whether it be a deeper and wider divergence or a closer convergence between the two ideas of mission, we would like to
offer some comments on three specific points which reveal a
certain weakness of the CWME in particular and of the WCC in
general.

There is, in the first place, an obsession with political and social structures and action which are identified as
Christian mission. The idea is to change everything that op-
presses man and the implication is that once those agents of
oppression disappear or are transformed, man will be really
free. As a result, one finds himself among people who speak
the same language and offer the same criticisms and solutions
of any leftist-oriented politician who praises Revolution (in
whatever terms it may be described), guerrillas and violence.
All evils come from Imperialism and all good will come with
the Revolution. The people who hold this view are not a majority but they are more vocal than the others who do not
take an extreme position. Although our words are not intended
as a condemnation of leftist ideas just because they are
leftist nor as a tacit approval of Imperialism (Mexico has
had its share of suffering in this regard), we do want to go
to the heart of the matter and declare that the approach of
the CWME is wrong because it forgets two things: 1) It will
do man no good if after he is liberated from those oppressing
structures he remains internally and spiritually the same
unregenerate man. 2) This was not the approach used by either
Christ or the apostles.

In regard to doing good, Christ had at his disposal far
greater means than any of us today: He could feed the poor
and heal the sick without the need to control the means of
production and without having to build hospitals. The apostles, and especially Paul who dealt more with Gentiles and
slaves, could have clamored for a political liberation and
for the destruction of structures like slavery and despotism
which were perhaps more oppressive then than they are now.
They saw, however, that the kingdom of God would not be fully
realized in this world and looked forward to an apocalyptic

consumation which apparently the WCC does not expect or perhaps does not consider relevant in view of man's poverty and
disease. What we say must not be taken as a sign that a
Christian must abstain from political participation, but
must be realistic in what he expects in this world and therefore must act according to sound priorities.

One would also think that some people from the CWME are
trying to impose these ideas on the Churches of the world,
but we can discern that up to now the Churches have obtained
only meager results. In fact, we have reason to believe that
even those people who deliberately and almost exclusively
adhere to this plan of action are obtaining meager results.
In the discussion of the Vietnam issue, an American delegate
very candidly admitted that there is a cleavage between the
left-oriented clergymen and the majority of the members of
their churches as indicated by the overwhelming reelection of
President Nixon. If in countries that enjoy absolute freedom and Churches have millions of members we see little results when the church or its clergymen engage in this type
of activity, what can we expect in countries where freedom is
restricted and the church is a tiny minority? Especially in
these latter cases the church must not dissipate its energy
in political or social action, but must give priority to its
main task which is gaining men and enrolling them in the kingdom of God.

Our second point has to do with a certain attitude, pre-
valent in WCC circles and very noticeable in Bangkok: It
wants to ignore or discredit the great ingatherings that are
taking place in many parts of the world, including the work
of thousands of missionaries *from the Third World*. The
millions who have become Protestants, especially Pentecostals,
in Latin America, the great number of converts among the Muslims in Indonesia, the phenomenal growth of the Kimbanguist
Church, which is itself a member of the WCC, etc., are dismissed as mere growth in numbers of members that has little
relevance to the task of the church. Although China was very
much in the delegates' mind and a special plenary session was
devoted to it, nobody would think of the 800 million Chinese
as likely candidates to accept the gospel nor would they think
that God can open a way so that many Christian churches can
be established there. In fact, when this possibility was
mentioned by the writer to a high official of the CWME, he
quickly snapped: "Leave the Chinese alone. They don't need
us." This is in line with the thinking in terms of a salvation in material and political terms and the idea, literally
expressed in the same session by an American delegate who said:
"Chairman Mao is God's Messiah to the Chinese." If they have
been liberated by Mao, apparently that is liberation enough
and they do not need the gospel.

This, in turn, takes us to our third point. As judged
by Bangkok, the WCC ignores the great opportunities that we
now have in regard to the gospel, the widespread hunger in
many souls for salvation in specific spiritual terms, in
relation to sinning men and a saving God. In actual fact the
meeting was permeated by pessimism, the feeling that we are
at the end of the missionary task as formerly conceived, the
idea that the church itself needs to be saved, which sounds
so strange to those who believe that Christians are the salt
of the earth.

THE FUNCTIONAL STRUCTURE

Our final observation has to do with the functioning of
the Conference as observed personally.

As is well known, the original core of member Churches
of the WCC was made up of Protestant Churches, and at the beginning it was thought of as a Protestant organization. This
is not so anymore because there are now Orthodox Churches that
belong. The Roman Catholic Church is not officially a member
of it and people wonder if it will ever join, but actually
this is not necessary, for at Bangkok there were Catholic
priests in practically every group, one of them directed the
meeting I have just mentioned on meditation, a nun was in
charge of the art workshop and at least one chaired a plenary
meeting. It was very interesting to notice that the representative from the Secretariat for Promoting Christian Unity
was more biblical in his speech to the meeting than were many
Protestants in their addresses.

We also wonder what the future holds for this organization
if, as has happened with Protestant organizations before, it
falls into the hands of radicals or people who are actually
divorced from the life of the Churches, but who at the same
time enjoy their financial support. When one sees on the
floor an activist from Central America who is interested in
nothing but "Revolution" or hears an avowed atheist from Italy
who practically makes a mockery of all religious beliefs but
at the same time, and according to the grapevine, is provided
with ecumenicals funds for several projects, one cannot help
but wonder what is coming next.

CONCLUSION

In conclusion and in all charity we can only say in our
personal response to the Salvation Today Conference that we
fully agree with Paul's estimate of the proclamation of Christ:

Some, indeed, proclaim Christ in a jealous and
quarrelsome spirit; others proclaim him in true
goodwill, and these are moved by love for me;
they know that it is to defend the Gospel that
I am where I am. But the others, moved by personal rivalry, present Christ from mixed motives,
meaning to stir up fresh trouble for me as I lie
in prison. What does it matter? One way or another, in pretence or sincerity, Christ is set
forth, and for that I rejoice. (Philippians
1:15-18. New English Bible).

However, we cannot help the feeling of dismay at the
theological direction the CWME seems inevitably following.
Knowing some of the participants personally, fully aware of
their earnestness and sincerity as well as their kindness,
it would be regrettable to find that their course is not
guided by the Word of God, for we cannot help but remember
also that anything that is not built on the solid rock of
God's Word will collapse.

5

Disneyland at Bangkok?

C. PETER WAGNER

One of the good things about the "Salvation Today" conference convened by the Commission on World Mission and Evangelism of the World Council of Churches at Bangkok, Thailand, December 29, 1972 through January 8, 1973, was that you could form your own opinion of it without much fear of being contradicted. No matter how the conference struck you, you were bound to find some who agreed as well as some who developed different points of view. Since your impression of the conference depended largely on which Bible study sessions and group interactions you attended, it is unlikely that any two of the 300-odd participants emerged with identical evaluations.

If I may be excused for a California analogy, Bangkok seemed to me to be an ecclesiastical Disneyland. Not only did the quaint curved roofs, the winding paths and the fancy landscaping remind one of Anaheim, but the impact the conference made on a person depended largely on the particular ride he happened to take. Some of the participants had good rides, and they are rather optimistic about the future course of

C. Peter Wagner is Associate Professor of Latin American Affairs at the Fuller Theological Seminary School of World Mission and Executive Director of the Fuller Evangelistic Association. He served as a missionary in Bolivia under the South America Mission and the Andes Evangelical Mission, 1956-71, and became Associate General Director of the latter. Among Wagner's most recent books are *Latin American Theology* (Eerdmans), *Frontiers in Missionary Strategy* (Moody), and *Church/Mission Tensions Today* (Moody).

the WCC/CWME. Mine, I'm sorry to report, were mediocre to poor.

The first bad ride came soon after I checked in. The conference had already been running for a few days. Several of my friends greeted me with the same question: "Did you hear what happened to Beyerhaus?" I soon heard that when, in the second session, German missiologist Peter Beyerhaus had suggested that the conference grapple seriously with the theological points raised in the Frankfurt Declaration, he was virtually declared out of order by WCC General Secretary Philip Potter himself. The conference newspaper reported Potter's saying that because the Frankfurt Declaration was produced by a particular group of Western German theologians, the CWME was prepared to discuss it in Germany, but not to share it as a world document. Potter's attack effectively tossed the issues of the "fundamental crisis of Christian mission" right out of Bangkok and back to Frankfurt.

Even before that, however, Potter had tackled another contemporary missiological issue, that of the "two billion." Fuller Seminary's Donald McGavran for several years had needled ecumenical leaders with the poignant question as to whether the two billion people in the world who have not yet had an opportunity to commit themselves to Jesus Christ would be betrayed by the conciliar movement. He had made the "two billion" a symbol in missiological circles, and had sharpened the debate between those who considered Christian mission as making disciples of these two billion in the classical sense and those who were more concerned with humanizing them by struggling to bring about a "shalom" of peace, justice and brotherhood.

Philip Potter dealt with the two billion like he dealt with the Frankfurt Declaration. In his opening address entitled, "Christ's Mission and Ours in Today's World," he brought up the matter of the debate on the two billion, then promptly dismissed it as "totally futile." His message reflected little sensitivity to such essential components of salvation doctrine as the depravity of the heart of man, the need for personal regeneration by the Spirit, and the eschatological realities of eternal life and eternal damnation. Instead, he dwelt on the Christian responsibility toward "the liberation of persons and societies from all that prevents them from living an authentic existence in justice and a shared community." Evangelicals could agree on the need for this social concern, but they were not willing to let it stand as the central objective of "Christ's mission and ours."

Having effectively muted the voices of McGavran (who was absent) and Beyerhaus (who was present), the conference was then forced to face the strong evangelical voice of Arthur Glasser, Dean of Fuller Seminary's School of World Mission, who had been invited as a "reflector." Glasser's "reflection," which was given by invitation in a later plenary session, rang loud and clear with evangelical content and evangelistic passion. When asked to flesh out his notes for *Evangelical Missions Quarterly*, he stayed up until the wee hours of the morning to write the piece below. Glasser's powerful delivery was a highlight of the conference, a good ride, but the leaders dealt with him in another way. The full-page mimeographed document summarizing that plenary session carried references to Rubem Alves' gloomy reflections on the sickness of Western culture, the despair of mankind and his own resulting hopelessness. It described other reflections on the servanthood and powerlessness of the church. But Glasser's biblical challenge rated not even a line!

A widely-publicized dialogue with Thai Buddhist leaders turned out to be a slow ride. Phra Maha Vorasak, an authority on Vipasana, advocated a "middle way." When he recommended that participants not drive their cars too fast, he drew a reaction from the social activists. When he commented that women in Thailand drive too slowly, the women's libbers protested. Evangelicals wished in vain that the dialogue would move from man's relationship to himself and other men to the subject of man's relationship to a living, personal God.

Ecumenical conference hoppers were of a general opinion that Bangkok marked a new era for Third World church leaders. Not only were they present and not only were they listened to, but it appeared that for the first time they were able to influence the course of a conference in a significant way. With Philip Potter, a West Indian, as General Secretary of the World Council of Churches, and Emilio Castro, a Uruguayan, installed at Bangkok as Director of the Commission on World Mission and Evangelism, there is little question that Third World leadership will yet increase as the years move by.

But whether this will help speed the fulfillment of the Great Commission and gather the harvest among the two billion remains to be seen. One of the serious structural problems of the Bangkok conference was that so few *missionaries* or *evangelists* participated in the meetings of the Commission on World *Mission* and *Evangelism*. Whether from the West or from the Third World, the predominant voices were those of *churchmen*, not missionaries. Their concerns were not so much winning those *outside* of the church, as housekeeping chores *within* the church. Bangkok was a living example of what I have called "The Babylonian Captivity of the Christian Mission."[1]

In a press conference, for example, three African leaders expressed their relief that the age of the missionary was finally over. When someone suggested that perhaps Africa could now send missionaries to the West, they shrugged off the idea with the comment that such a request seemed to them to be a thinly-disguised obsession of guilt-ridden Westerners, and that it is clearly the wrong track for the future.

Some of the unplanned side shows reflected feelings of churchmen which appear to be running deep in some circles. The morning after a meeting on China, for example, a large poster appeared on the public bulletin board with this text: "At China meeting — did you notice the compulsive neurosis of the West to 'convert' China? Salvation — God *save* China from 'conversion.' "

One Third World leader, in a group meeting, expressed an opinion that was fairly widespread concerning the attitude of the Western, especially American, participants. He was visibly disturbed by what he described as the "masochistic feeling" of Americans there. "Hit me, hit me!" he heard the Americans saying. "We're not yet saved!" Tongue-in-cheek, he questioned the efficacy of self-flagellation as a soteriological option.

All the rides weren't that bad. The final report of Sub-Section III-B, "Growing Churches and Renewal," stands out as a landmark like the snow-capped peak of Disneyland's Matterhorn. It mentions "the proclamation of the Gospel of Jesus Christ to all the world so that, by responding to him, persons and their situations may be saved." The whole sub-section report is a plea for a return of the church to biblical evangelism. It was no coincidence that Arthur Glasser, Peter Beyerhaus, and Bishop Chandu Ray, along with other evangelicals, were actively involved in that section.

[1]A 13-page mimeographed paper with this title is available from the Fuller Theological Seminary School of World Mission, 135 North Oakland Ave., Pasadena, CA 91101, upon request.

These men, joined by Bishop Manuel Gaxiola of Mexico, Donald Hoke, Harold Lindsell, and several others of like mind, made their presence felt. A ray of evangelical concern does shine through, even in the final "Letter to the Churches." It reaffirms salvation in the name of Jesus Christ, and states that "through the work of the Holy Spirit we have recognized together the power of salvation by his cross as it is manifest in his resurrection." One of the official resolutions pledges the CWME to "press efforts at all levels to understand the concerns and consider the implications of the performance in mission of conservative evangelicals both within and without the membership of the WCC." The official news release recognizes that "the presence of conservative evangelicals and proponents of the Frankfurt Declaration point to a new dialogue of what mission really is."

When the CWME finally decides "what mission really is," will they change course and return to biblical priorities? Will they distinctly persuade the member churches to dedicate time, energy, budget, and personnel to a renewed effort to turn men and women from idols to serve the living and true God (1 Thess. 1:9)? Will they clearly offer the Bread of Life right along with the bread of development and justice? Will they adopt Jesus' priorities which he articulated in terms of "not laboring for the food which perisheth, but for that food which endureth unto everlasting life" (Jn. 6:27)?

If the conciliar movement is truly interested in the concerns of conservative evangelicals, they will come to grips with these and a score of other equally penetrating questions. At this point I am not willing to predict which way the WCC/CWME will go in the years to come. Recent history would lead one to guess that the biblical emphasis on mission and evangelism, prominent at Edinburgh at the beginning of the century, will continue to be stifled. However, a new spiritual awakening, being felt increasingly in many parts of the world, produces a degree of hope. If we can do nothing else, we can pray sincerely for our brethren in the conciliar movement at this crucial juncture of their history and ours.

6

Salvation Isn't
the Same Today

BANGKOK CONSULTATION

DONALD HOKE

Theological confusion on the theme itself, "Salvation Today," marked the international conference sponsored by the Commission on World Mission and Evangelism (CWME) of the World Council of Churches. The two-week session ended in Bangkok, Thailand, last month amid a plethora of pronouncements but, in the words of an evangelical participant, "with no clear or definitive statements on the meaning of salvation today, yesterday, or tomorrow." Widely diverse opinions offered on the floor and in smaller work groups ranged from left-wing Marxism to conservative evangelicalism.

The conference brought together more than 200 representatives of churches in nearly seventy countries to "celebrate salvation as a gift of God through the Holy Spirit and . . . consider what are the implications of salvation today for the life of the churches and the ecumenical movement." About 40 per cent were from third-world nations. An estimated 10 per cent were staffers of the WCC, the National Council of Churches, and the East Asia Christian Conference (EACC). It was the seventh such meeting held by the CWME since 1910; the last was in Mexico City in 1963.

Layman M. M. Thomas of the Mar Thoma Church of India, chairman of the WCC's Central Committee, showed in his opening speech which way the WCC leadership was headed in its interpretation of the theme. Said he:

> The primary concern of the Christian mission is . . . with the salvation of human spirituality, with man's right choices in the realm of self-transcendence, and with structures of ultimate meaning and sacredness—not in any pietistic or individualistic isolation, but in relation to and expressed within the material, social, and cultural revolutions of our time.

In short, the mission of the church "is to be present within the creative liberation movements of our time," he declared.

WCC general secretary Philip Potter endorsed Thomas's views, expanding the liberation angle and lashing out at the social sins of the West, particularly America's role in the Viet Nam conflict. (Potter was formerly head of the CWME. As such, he was the chief architect of the Bangkok consultation.)

Concluding that "salvation in Christ . . . is concerned with the liberation of persons and societies from all that prevents them from living an authentic existence in justice and a shared community," Potter declared that "the church itself needs to be saved, liberated from all that is false to the revolutionary, convicting, and renewing nature of the Gospel." Even the church is a mission field, he said, because of its "racial, economic, and cultural captivity."

Dialogue as the major contemporary method of expressing the church's mission found frequent mention in the program from Potter's opening remarks on. One group visited a Buddhist temple to have dialogue with the monks there. But when the general secretary of the Church of Thailand gave a stirring report of how revival had broken out in the Buddhist land, resulting in a doubled conversion rate in the past year, a German delegate reacted negatively. "Very bad," he scowled. The revivalistic theology of the Thai church and the enumeration of "so many souls saved" slaps the whole dialogue program in the face, he said.

The presence of invited evangelicals early projected controversy into the plenary "open hearing." Missions and ecumenics professor Peter Beyerhaus at Germany's Tübingen University requested the floor in order to protest the polarization of ecumenism and evangelicalism since the 1963 sessions in Mexico City. Declaring that an "infection of faith" was spreading throughout the world, he charged that the WCC and the CWME had not responded to the Wheaton and Berlin congresses and the 1970 Frankfurt Declaration (an evangelical missions statement) with any positive affirmation of the nature of contemporary evangelism and missions. He suggested that the conference consider the declaration.

Response was varied, almost all negative, ranging from assertions that the problem was one of biblical hermeneutics and semantics to an African's statement that he was disgusted with such attempts to foist controversies of the West on the third world. Batak churchman Sorita Nababan from Indonesia complained that the Frankfurt Declaration (Beyerhaus was a chief architect) had become a center of controversy in some areas of his church. Potter insisted that the WCC had responded to the declaration by running articles on it in a mission journal. Meanwhile, Beyerhaus argued in vain that consideration of a biblically based statement is not imposition of a Western controversy.

A Dutch delegate in the plenary meeting proposed immediate chartering of a plane to take at least 100 delegates to North Viet Nam to identify with the suffering and death caused by U. S. bombs there. The conference settled instead for a statement, overwhelmingly passed, calling on the WCC to send a team of leaders to North Viet Nam as a gesture of solidarity, and asking churches everywhere to pray "for the conversion of the power-deluded politicals" responsible for the Indochina turmoil. The rhetoric throughout the resolution was decidedly anti-American.

There were other politically oriented statements, an expression of "concern regarding relationships between conservative evangelical groups and churches traditionally related to conciliar groupings," and—almost laughably—an offer to help with the evangelical Congress on World Evangelization to be held in Lausanne, Switzerland, in July, 1974.

A work section led by Uruguayan Methodist Emilio Castro, who succeeded Potter as head of the CWME, rationalized:

> Our concentration upon the social, economic, and political implications of the Gospel does not in any way deny the personal and eternal dimensions of salvation. Rather, we would emphasize that the personal, social, individual, and corporate aspects of salvation are so inter-related that they are inseparable.

What was left unsaid was perhaps more significant than what was said. There was no call for justice and liberation of the subjugated people in Iron Curtain countries, no adequate recognition of the evangelical revolution (the international spread of the Jesus movement, revival in many lands, Key 73, Explo '72, the congresses on evangelism, the surging Pentecostal phenomenon), and no emphasis on reaching the world's two billion people without Christ.

With the exception of a few lone voices raised in small sections and Bible studies, the concept of salvation as the redemption of the individual from sin unto eternal life through faith in a crucified, risen redeemer was not sounded. During the open hearing, a bearded Copt in robes spoke up quietly: "I am fearful that the church will forget salvation by the blood of Christ . . . and I am concerned about reaching non-Christians around the world."

His was the plaintive voice of one crying in a seeming wilderness of organized Christendom.

7

What Evangelicals
Can Learn From Bangkok

What's primary in the salvation Christ offers men and women?
Is our traditional answer adequate?
Missionary statesman Arthur F. Glasser explains what the recent ecumenical conference in Bangkok, Thailand, contributed to this much-debated issue.

As 1973 opened, church leaders from around the world gathered in Bangkok, Thailand, to discuss "Salvation Today." Sponsored by the Commission on World Mission and Evangelism of the World Council of Churches, the ecumenical assembly sought to define salvation in a twentieth-century context.

Of course, the conclusions of the gathering have profound implications for missionary enterprises.

What is this salvation that Christians have been called to proclaim?

Are conservatives who stress its spiritual aspects or liberals who concentrate on the material aspects more accurate in their understanding of it?

Dr. Arthur F. Glasser, consulting editor of ETERNITY *Magazine and dean of the Fuller Theological Seminary School of World Mission, was specially invited to be an observer at the Bangkok gathering.*

Shortly after his return, William J. Petersen, executive editor of ETERNITY *Magazine, interviewed him:*

Petersen: Dr. Glasser, why was "Salvation Today" selected as theme of this worldwide conference?

Glasser: Well, it was selected because in many parts of the church today there is great uncertainty about what salvation means. The uncertainties run so deep that many church leaders are openly wondering why they should put forth the effort to proclaim "salvation" all over the world.

Petersen: If church leaders are uncertain about what salvation is, you can hardly expect the non-Christian to know what it is.

Glasser: Exactly. And besides that, I think that the ecumenical leaders were hoping that a serious conference on the theme of salvation might help break down the cold war between evangelicals and the ecumenical movement.

Petersen: Do you feel the participants in the Bangkok conference grappled seriously with the theme?

Glasser: Not really. Actually, many different points of view were represented. Those from East Europe, for instance, were not concerned about making converts but in how to live in a society that is totally secular and which denies their children any religious education. For many of those in the Third World—Africa, Latin America and Asia—salvation means liberation from social structures that enslave them.

Petersen: But what about the traditional missionary viewpoint?

Glasser: Well, of course, most missionary leaders see salvation as God's gift to those who are converted to Christ. For them, the missionary task is bringing people face to face with Jesus Christ.

Petersen: The debate must have been pretty vigorous.

Glasser: It certainly was. As a matter of fact, the debate really had been going on for the past four years. Long before we met at Bangkok, books and articles had been written, and conferences and debates were held in various parts of the world. The leaders wanted Bangkok to be a time for celebration of salvation rather than further study.

Petersen: Did many evangelicals attend?

Glasser: I was one of 12 conservative evangelicals who were specially invited.

Petersen: Were you the only conservatives in attendance?

Glasser: Oh no. A surprising number of men in the ecumenical movement are basically conservative in their theology. And the 12 of us from outside the ecumenical movement appreciated their role in the Bangkok conference very much.

Petersen: I'd like to know a little more about the composition of the delegates. Who was actually there?

Glasser: Well, I think that is quite important. It helps you evaluate the entire conference. Of the 326 who gathered at Bangkok about 50% were from Africa, Asia and South America. Quite a number came from Eastern Europe and the Soviet Union.

But even more significant than the geographical representation was the ecclesiastical aspect. Approximately 20% were World Council staff members from Geneva, Switzerland, or

". . . only 8% were missionaries or missionary directors."

from the ecumenical hierarchy all over the world. Fully 50% were church officials and leaders of various denominations.

Petersen: Would these men be related to the missionary branch of their churches?

Glasser: No, few of these men were directly involved in the missionary organizational end of their churches. In fact, I talked with several, including a bishop or two, who appeared to know very little about the problems facing missions and churches throughout the world today. And yet, they were voting delegates in a top-level conference ostensibly devoted to "world mission" and "evangelism."

As for the rest, about 15% were theologians from various schools, 7% were Roman Catholic observers and only 8% were missionaries or mission directors.

Petersen: In other words, although this was a conference on missions, missionaries were a small minority.

Glasser: Definitely. And when you think of the thousands and thousands of missionaries all over the world, they were really poorly represented at Bangkok. In fact some people at the outset said it would be a washout, the eclipse of mission, the absorption

of mission by the churches.

Petersen: Do you agree that this conference represented the desire of the church to dominate missions?

Glasser: Yes, I am afraid it was. But to get the right perspective, we need to go back to the great conference of mission leaders that was convened in Edinburgh, Scotland.

Petersen: That would be the World Missionary Conference of 1910?

Glasser: Yes. At that time the missionary movement was advancing all over the world. But there were problems of competition and duplication between missions. Also, as new churches came into being, there was the question of their relationship to the missions. So missionary leaders decided that they would come together and discuss their problems.

From that conference, two streams of organizational life emerged: one, the purely missionary stream, came to be known as the International Missionary Council, and the other was the churchly stream. The IMC had some significant missionary conferences—Jerusalem in 1928, Madras in 1938, Whitby, Ont., in 1947, Willingen in 1952, Ghana in 1958. At these conferences they talked primarily about the great world outside, where people were without the knowledge of Jesus Christ. The stated aim of the IMC was "the proclamation of the Gospel of Jesus Christ to the whole world to the end that all men might believe in Him and might be saved."

Petersen: The churchly stream that you mentioned eventually became the

World Council of Churches, didn't it?

Glasser: Yes, the World Council of Churches was formed at Amsterdam in 1948.

Petersen: And how did these two streams ever happen to merge together?

Glasser: Well, because the church is always thinking about its people becoming better Christians in their daily lives, and missions are always talking about the regions beyond, some of the leaders started to wonder if perhaps this represented a false dichotomy between church and mission. Isn't everything that the church does a missionary activity? Isn't every Christian a missionary and every church a mission? Why should we have an elite group doing our work for us? Besides, if the missions have brought into being churches overseas, maybe the era for mission per se has come to an end now that we have a worldwide church. (That's how they reasoned.)

Petersen: So, we heard the slogan, "The church is mission."

Glasser: Right. And this led to the fusion in 1961 at New Delhi of the IMC into the World Council of Churches. In time, the missionary concern of the WCC came to be known as the Division of World Mission and Evangelism. Still later it became merely a Commission.

Petersen: Now, many evangelicals were quite concerned about this merger at the time.

Glasser: Yes, and the reasons, of course, are obvious. Would the church absorb mission? Would the missionary concern of the church be eclipsed by churchly concerns?

Petersen: What happened?

Glasser: Well, in 1963, the Division of World Mission and Evangelism had a conference in Mexico City, and in that conference they started to reflect on their aim, that all people might be saved. The question was asked, "What is the form and content of the salvation that Christ offers men and women in the secular world?" But as they reflected on it they realized that they would not be able to do more than touch the border of this subject. "We'll have to grapple with it at our next meeting," they said.

Petersen: And the next meeting didn't come for ten years?

Glasser: Yes, and to some this long delay was evidence of a waning concern for the millions in this world who are without Jesus Christ.

Petersen: So, I suppose you didn't know what to expect when you got to Bangkok.

Glasser: Not quite. Although I wanted to be hopeful, I feared the worst. I recognized the privilege of being invited to attend. But I was deeply distressed by some of the pre-Bangkok studies on "Salvation Today" that came from the WCC headquarters in Geneva, Switzerland. One text, "Salvation Today and Contemporary Experience," spoke of being saved by Mao and on the next page it spoke of being saved by Jesus. Many contributors did not seem to accept any difference between Christians and non-Christians. They seemed uncertain as to whether salvation was by faith in Jesus Christ or whether it was by participation in the struggle for justice.

Petersen: Salvation was equated with liberation?

Glasser: Well, yes, and missions seemed to mean that you would give yourself to the struggle to help others and humanize others.

Petersen: But then what happened after you arrived in Bangkok?

Glasser: Well, fortunately this book was quite ignored, and I began to sense a change. In fact, it appeared that things had begun to change even before that. A surprisingly high number of the delegates wrote in advance that they wanted to participate in the Bible studies. So, the planners had to rearrange the program and form three new major Bible study groups of 22 to 24 members each. But when they organized this larger number of Bible studies, they were running a risk. Because, you and I know that God, through the Scripture, does His own thing.

Well, the conference began with three days in which from 8:00 in the morning until 12:00 noon small groups gathered around the Word of God. And there was no playing games with one another. Our differences were real, and the passions were manifest, and arguments at times were rather bluntly presented, but I cannot but feel that we all grappled fairly with many biblical categories related to salvation.

It happened that in the Bible study group with which I was associated, we decided to draft our own affirmation of salvation today. And it was presented to the entire assembly and was accepted almost without debate.

Petersen: That's great.

Glasser: It was amazing. We were so diverse and yet through the hours spent studying the Bible, we were brought to deep agreement on many fundamental truths.

Petersen: But you have indicated that many of the missionary concerns of previous conferences were pretty well forgotten at Bangkok.

Glasser: Yes. I would say that there were three major differences between this conference and previous IMC conventions.

First, there was a shift from the old IMC emphasis on preaching the Gospel, persuading men to believe and planting churches. Instead, the emphasis was on the "cultural mandate."

Petersen: What do you mean by that?

Glasser: Well, in Scripture there are two mandates; the evangelistic mandate and the cultural mandate. Salvation really has implications for both. According to the cultural mandate, God desires to involve men in accepting responsibility for the world. He is concerned about the poor, the oppressed, the weak. He is concerned about government, injustice, oppression and so on. At Bangkok, this cultural mandate was central, rather than the evangelistic mandate.

Petersen: Do you believe in a cultural mandate?

Glasser: I certainly do. If the whole Bible is the Word of God, obviously there is a place for the Old Testament prophet as well as the New Testament evangelist. There is a prophetic dimension to the Gospel, but I certainly don't want to forget the evangelistic dimension as they did at Bangkok.

Petersen: How else was Bangkok different from previous international conferences?

Glasser: Well, they tried by demonstration to show us their new thing in evangelism. They called it "dialogue." At a plenary session we sat back and watched several WCC experts "dialogue" with some local Buddhist priests. This was to show the respect Christians should have for other religions and to prove that Christianity has much to learn from them.

But it fell flat. Jesus Christ and Salvation Today were not mentioned. Dr. Hans J. Margull, professor of missions and ecumenics at Hamburg University, tried to save the pieces by pointing out that in encounters of this sort, whereas you start with religious questions, in time you move to matters pertaining to the realities of human community, and finally end up talking about man. Man, not God, becomes central.

Petersen: That certainly undercuts Christian missionary work.

Glasser: Right. Furthermore, it seemed to me that this attempt at interreligious dialogue was a distinct affront to our host church, the Church of Christ of Thailand. At the communion service early in the conference, the Rev. Wichean Watakeecharoen, who is general secretary of that church body, preached a great sermon on Isaiah 53 and Romans 5. And he also reported that many parts of his country were witnessing large numbers of youth and older people making the decision to accept Jesus Christ as their Savior. "The aim of the Church of Christ of Thailand," he said, "is to double its

membership during the four-year period from 1970 to 1974. At the present time in Thailand there are many young preachers whom God is using in the work of evangelism. Their preaching is a clear witness of Jesus Christ. As they preach, they invite all who have never received Jesus Christ as their Savior to stand up and acknowledge Him publicly. . . . The Holy Spirit is at work in His church."

Petersen: I would think that such a statement would have some effect on the delegates.

Glasser: I think it did. Here was a demonstration of something infinitely superior to dialogue. Something biblical! Buddhists coming to Jesus Christ!

Petersen: Well, what was the third trend at Bangkok?

Glasser: Way back in 1947 at the Whitby Conference in Canada, the slogan was "Partnership in Obedience." The idea was that churches and missions are partners and are not to compete with one another. We're not going to downgrade one another, but we're going to link arms. At Bangkok, the centrality of the church came through. There was no thought of mission. In fact, there was an almost total lack of awareness that large numbers of people in the world today are still without the knowledge of Jesus Christ. I can appreciate the churchly concerns of churches. But I had a hard time accepting the "brush off" given on occasion to those whose concerns are for missionary outreach. It was tragic to watch a leader in the East Asian Christian Council dismiss as meddling the concern of European and American Lutherans for the Chinese people. I couldn't help but recall Bishop Stephen Neill's pointed observation: "Some small younger churches are, in theory, 'the church' of a very wide area which they may have neither the strength nor the inclination to evangelize. . . . Indeed . . . younger church leaders sometimes give the impression that they would rather that their fellow-countrymen die as heathen than that they should be brought to the knowledge of Christ by Christians from the West."

Petersen: Did you talk theology and social action all day long and every day?

Glasser: Almost! But there were some diversions. One night they showed us the film *Marjoe*, the documentary of a discredited Pentecostal evangelist. I felt ashamed. My good friend Bishop Manuel J. Gaxiola of Mexico, a Pentecostal, was also a delegate. How he must have felt to see the only representation of gospel preaching in the evangelical sense portrayed as a mockery of his own church.

Petersen: On what note, then, did the conference end?

Glasser: Well, this was one of the most amazing things of all. They invited a representative of the Vatican secretariat, Father Jerome Haber, an American, to evaluate the meetings. He got up and spoke in French and when it was translated, I couldn't but blink my eyes. What he said was something like this, "I am appalled that you people can discuss 'Salvation Today,' day after day, and all its ramifications, but not listen to what the Apostle Paul said about it. I haven't heard anyone speak on justification by faith. I've heard no one speak of everlasting life. What about God's righteous wrath against sin?" Well, I felt this was my brother in Christ speaking.

Petersen: What would you say evangelicals can learn from Bangkok?

Glasser: Well, on the positive level, I think we should get a new appreciation that salvation is not just something that Christ accomplished for us on the cross in the past, nor is it something that is strictly eschatological, a salvation in the future when Christ shall appear. Jesus Christ wants to save us now. We do have an Old Testament

prophetic responsibility to present-day society. As an evangelical, I cannot stand against what the Bible says about my responsibility in relation to government, to war, to racism, and so forth. Just as the World Council has forgotten the evangelistic mandate, so evangelicals have often forgotten the cultural mandate. The Bible says we are to be salt in the earth. This isn't modernism; it's the Word of God. We are to let Jesus Christ save us from being captured by the status quo, from being selfish, from participating in those societal activities that dehumanize others.

Petersen: Next year, evangelicals are going to be involved in the International Congress on World Evangelization at Lausanne, Switzerland. This is the one that Billy Graham is promoting. What are the implications of the Bangkok meeting for evangelicals as they meet at Lausanne?

Glasser: Well, Lausanne is obviously going to be a necessary corrective to Bangkok. I am certain it will have a better representation of evangelists, missionaries and pastors who are concerned with evangelism and missions. The delegates will largely be from the Third World. In fact, it could be a sort of Edinburgh II and stress the urgency of sharing the Gospel with the two million who have never yet heard it. So I am sure Lausanne will stress the evangelistic mandate and that's vitally important.

Petersen: But you're concerned that Lausanne may neglect the cultural mandate?

Glasser: Yes, I'm afraid that just as Bangkok neglected the evangelistic mandate, so Lausanne may neglect the cultural mandate. Recently, Billy Graham said, "I'm a New Testament evangelist, not an Old Testament prophet." I fully appreciate what he said. This was his evaluation of his gifts. And yet, this antithesis can be misunderstood. In certain situations, Old Testament prophets are as important as New Testament evangelists. At Lausanne the leaders will have to remind the delegates that evangelicals are under obligation to proclaim the messages of the Old Testament prophets. After all, the Old Testament is in the Bible, too.

Petersen: One last question, Dr. Glasser. What do you think of the future of mission in the ecumenical movement?

Glasser: Well, the Bangkok meeting was called by the Commission of World Mission and Evangelism, but actually, the words, "world mission and evangelism" didn't convey much meaning in Bangkok. And I believe that this part of the World Council of Churches will continue to diminish in size and influence. Churchly concerns will continue to dominate. Biblical evangelism will continue to fade in WCC circles. The WCC is simply too preoccupied with power and influence in the secular sense. The leaders will try to exert power in the interest of humanizing society. And there is a validity to this. But it won't be the power of the Gospel as we know it. If there was any theme that was almost entirely absent from the Bangkok deliberations, it was the Person and Work of the Holy Spirit. □

PART III

Post-Bangkok Reflections

8

TWO EVANGELICALS LOOK AT THE BANGKOK CONSULTATION

❝❝ MORE HORIZONTAL THAN VERTICAL ❞❞
by C. Peter Wagner

Over 300 churchmen of all colors gathered December 29-January 8 in Bangkok, Thailand in a quest for a contemporary meaning of salvation. Under the theme "Salvation Today" these men and women, called together by the World Council of Churches' Commission on World Mission and Evangelism, participated in Bible studies, group discussions, plenary sessions and worship services. They diligently attempted to agree, at least in a measure, as to what is the mission of the church in today's world.

Evangelicals had hoped that the Bangkok meeting would be a watershed in missions focusing the thrust of the conciliar movement once again on biblical evangelism and Great Commission missions. It could have sounded a clarion call to churches all over the world to rise to the challenge of the two billion-plus people on this planet who have not yet committed themselves to Jesus Christ. It could have become a launching pad from which a renewed missionary force would move out to proclaim the gospel of salvation to all nations.

Cultural Mandate to the Fore

Political, social and economic concerns, however, seemed to draw the spotlights. Delegates appeared more inclined to promote social justice than to avoid the final judgment. Although evangelicals there were willing to concede that the Bible contains a cultural mandate, they insisted that the evangelistic mandate be given at least

Arthur F. Glasser is Dean of the School of World Mission at Fuller Theological Seminary in Pasadena, California. On the same faculty, C. Peter Wagner is also Executive Director of the Fuller Evangelistic Association.

equal time, but to little avail. The Vietnam war, white racism, and technological progress came under heavy and persistent attack. The Chinese cultural revolution was praised for its liberating effects and one delegate even referred to Mao as a "messiah."

Evangelicals were politely listened to, but for every word that stressed the urgency of men and women being reconciled to God, 100 seemed directed to the horizontal dimensions of the gospel. When, in a plenary session, German missiologist Peter Beyerhaus recommended that the assembly come to grips with the theological issues raised in the well-publicized Frankfurt Declaration, he was immediately challenged by none other than WCC General Secretary Philip Potter. Potter disallowed the Frankfurt Declaration as a topic for discussion on the grounds that it represented the views of a limited group of German theologians and therefore did not qualify as a world document.

One of the clearest pleas for an understanding of salvation today in terms of atonement through Christ's shed blood and forgiveness of sins was given by the Dean of Fuller Seminary's School of World Mission, Arthur Glasser. His address from the floor drew significant applause from the assembly. However, the next day's document summarizing that plenary session mentioned items such as the sickness of Western culture and the powerlessness of the Church, but reference to Glasser's presentation was conspicuously absent.

One African leader stated with feeling that now that the African church has gained full autonomy, the age of the missionary is over once and for all. Little effort was made to reconcile such an attitude with Christ's commission to make disciples of all nations, or with the sobering fact that two and a half billion people who are not yet Christians desperately need salvation today.

Joyous Reports from the Third World

Happily not all Third World leaders agreed that the age of the missionary is over. Bishop Chandu Ray of Singapore gave evangelical leadership, along with Glasser and others, to the subsection on church growth and renewal. There men from Madagascar, Korea, Indonesia, and Taiwan shared their experiences of seeing thousands come to Christ and churches overflowing. It did not occur to any of them that missionaries are no longer needed. The report of this group shines like a ray of bright sunshine among the final Bangkok documents.

Evangelicals left Bangkok unconvinced that salvation is more horizontal than vertical and that the missionary task of the church is obsolete. It did become painfully apparent to many observers that leadership in Great Commission missions will in all probability not come from the WCC/CWME in the foreseeable future, although some participants felt more optimistic. Evangelicals will now need to rally their forces on all six continents as never before so that the world might hear the clear gospel message.

❝❝ DEEP FEELINGS OF AMBIVALENCE ❞❞
by Arthur F. Glasser

How should a conservative evangelical evaluate the recent Bangkok Congress on "Salvation Today?" Inasmuch as it was convened by a Commission on World Mission and Evangelism, he might work his way through its official documents, select themes related to "mission" and "evangelism" and reflect on their adequacy. For instance, he would find that the Congress affirmed:

> Each generation must evangelize its own generation. To work for church growth and renewal is the chief, abiding and irreplaceable task of Christian mission.

Right on! The task is to win non-Christians to Jesus Christ, multiply congregations, labor for renewal among the people of God. How central to Christian mission!

But what about "Salvation Today?" Did the delegates really agree on what it is all about? Were they not representative of the theologically pluralistic constituency that makes up the World Council of Churches? Quite true, and yet on the last day, before parting they adopted an "Affirmation of Salvation Today" that contained the following:

With gratitude and joy we affirm again our confidence in the sufficiency of our crucified and risen Lord. We know Him as the one who is, and who was, and who is to come, the sovereign Lord of all. To the individual He comes with power to liberate him from every evil and sin, from every power in heaven and earth, and from every threat of life or death.

To the world He comes as the Lord of the universe, with deep compassion for the poor and the hungry, to liberate the powerless and the oppressed and to liberate the powerful and oppressors in judgment and mercy.

He calls his church to be part of his saving activity both in calling men to decisive personal response to his Lordship, and in unequivocal commitment to movements and works by which all men may know justice and have opportunity to be fully human.

One might gather, then, that this Congress marked a distinct triumph for historic biblical Christianity. Alas, this was hardly the case. Evangelicals who attended its 11 days of protracted debate and participated in the Third Assembly of the CWME that followed (four more days!) came away with deep feelings of ambivalence.

Much to Admire

On the one hand, there was much to admire. The conveners were courageous. They were determined not to manipulate its 300 delegates with a heavy succession of canned speeches. Rather, they scheduled the major parts of three successive days—from eight A.M. till noon—to group Bible study. Indeed, they organized three additional study groups at the last minute, because the delegates wanted it this way. More than 50 percent of the delegates came from the Third World. Their witness confirmed what we had earlier suspected: many of the Ecumenical Movement in Africa, Asia, and Latin America were evangelical in faith and obedience, especially the French-speaking Africans. I had underestimated the vigor of French Protestant missions and their loyalty to the biblical faith of the Reformation. The leaders of the churches they planted spoke well of Jesus Christ.

On the other hand, evangelicals cannot but be critical of many of Bangkok's emphases. As a result one wonders as to the future of the CWME and its related agencies. Originally, as the *International Missionary*

Council, this stream of concern embraced most major missionary agencies. Its stated aim was biblical—nothing less than the evangelization of the world. But through merging with the World Council of Churches (in 1961) this stream tended to be mixed with other concerns. Over the years the missionary presence in the WCC has dwindled, even on the level of organization it has diminished from a "Division" to a "Commission."

Neither missionaries nor evangelists were much in evidence at Bangkok. Delegate composition was 20 percent WCC/CWME staff, 50 percent church officials, 15 percent theologians, seven percent Roman Catholics, and eight percent mission-related personnel. Bangkok represented the latest demonstration in the long history of the Church: when churchmen dominate missions, they reduce their significance with the naive deduction that "the Church is mission" and soon forget the world outside. Popes and bishops rarely launch evangelistic or missionary movements.

Pitiable Islands of Diminishing Commitment

What of the future? Bangkok clearly revealed that many European and North American mainline churches are not really indigenous to the 1970's, either as "missionary" or "saving" institutions. That these churches are failing to grow not only points to the theological malaise of their leadership but also to their lack of vital relationship to contemporary culture. Too often these churches represent pitiable islands of diminishing commitment to the Biblical gospel or outmoded cultural expressions of "ghetto" Christianity.

In my judgment, the only hope for the evangelization of this generation lies in those evangelical movements which irrespective of ecclesiastical linkage are facing outward and sensing the shame that over two billion in the world today need to hear the gospel of Jesus Christ. They shall be drawn to the emphases of the 1974 Lausanne *International Congress on World Evangelization.* Thank God for them! But more, evangelicals should not be so superficial and parochial that they dismiss Bangkok with an impatient wave of the hand. The

Church has a biblically defined *cultural mandate* that she can neglect only to her peril. Many of its positive elements were affirmed at Bangkok. Bangkok's flaw was in identifying the "cultural mandate" with "world mission" and "evangelism."

The Church also has a biblically defined *evangelistic mandate* that she must carry out if the nations are to be won to faith in Christ. Lausanne, under God, must affirm this task as pointedly and vigorously as possible.

Let us face it: at their best, churches throughout the world today represent light and darkness, truth and error, wheat and tares. They also represent diversity and incompleteness in their understanding and performance of the Christian mission. If we accept one another and seek to express, wherever possible, our unity in Christ, the gospel of reconciliation will be proclaimed to this generation and social justice will be furthered in the earth. However, only by exercising a pastoral care for one another can this total task be accomplished. There is the sense in which *Lausanne '74* can build upon *Bangkok '73*.

9

Salvation - yesterday, tomorrow, and today

This speech by Arthur Glasser was written and delivered in the heat of the battle, from the floor of the plenary session of the Bangkok "Salvation Today" conference, January 4, 1973, on request of the conference leadership. In it Glasser reflects on his personal findings during the previous three days of unhurried study of a series of biblical texts prescribed for all participants. Evangelicals will be pleased that such an eloquent statement of biblical truth was heard in this crucial ecumenical gathering.

ARTHUR F. GLASSER

Mr. Chairman:

When approached to disclose to this conference my inner wrestlings of heart and conscience rising from this fresh exposure to the Word of God, and to the voices and concerns of my brothers and sisters, my first instinct was to draw back. What could I possibly say? Whereas I am most grateful for the privilege of bearing witness, I am also painfully aware that we are still in mid-passage, insofar as our investigation of "Salvation Today" is concerned. However, upon learning of the emphases to be made shortly by the other two reflectors (Bethuel A. Kiplagat of the Sudan Council of Churches and Rubem Alves of Brazil), I felt that I should respond by bearing witness to the manner in which the biblical texts, to which we have all been exposed, have spoken to my heart.

I desire to be positive. Actually, I am constrained — although the comparison is invidious — to identify myself with the Apostle Paul and his confession of faith and hope in the midst of a stormy sea and impending shipwreck (Acts 27). How hopeless was his situation. How like our world today! Such a troubled sea! We look out to its horizons and see so much

Arthur F. Glasser is Dean of the Fuller Theological Seminary School of World Mission and Institute of Church Growth. Previously he served as a navy chaplain, a missionary to China under the Overseas Missionary Fellowship, and as Home Director for North America of the O.M.F. He is co-author (with Eric S. Fife) of *Missions in Crisis* (Inter-Varsity Press), and his writings are familiar to readers of evangelical periodicals and scholarly journals.

hatred and wrath, so much greed and misery, and such unwarranted racial pride. And the ecological crisis is mounting. We've polluted the air, defiled the water, and are squandering the resources of the world God has given us. When we reflect on the City of Man which we have built, we want to weep even as Jesus wept over Jerusalem. But let me attempt to sound a note of hope. As Paul confessed his faith in God and in God's superintending providence, so I would call you to be of good cheer. In the midst of our powerlessness, God is! And He is at work!

Liberation in Egypt

Recall the Exodus event. We began our study with the covenant people of God, their lives made bitter by economic exploitation, political oppression and cultural disintegration. I am afraid we were directed to focus overmuch on peripheral agents of liberation: the civil disobedience of the midwives and the violent protest of Moses, who in his passionate advocacy of justice, slew an Egyptian and hid his body in the sand.

What impressed me in a new way were not the acts of men nor even the plagues with which God shattered the economic structure of the Egyptians. Deliverance did not come through acts of personal courage or spectacular displays of power. Rather, victory came through powerlessness. I saw in a new way the centrality of the slain lamb, its blood splattered on doorposts and lintel, and the angel of the Lord separating by judgment the people of God from their oppressors. Here was the mystery of powerlessness overcoming power through the suffering of death. There was the triumph of appropriating faith.

Now, what abiding symbol comes to us from that dramatic record of "salvation yesterday?" The clenched fist? The bandoleer over the shoulder and the upraised rifle? Not at all! Rather, the symbol of a lamb that had been slain. This was what caught the imagination of the Apostle Paul. Recall what he said: "Christ our Paschal Lamb has been sacrificed" (1 Cor. 5:7).

The Sufferer in the Psalms

Together, we studied Psalm 22. We confronted its unknown sufferer. In his powerlessness he plumbed the depths of physical, social and spiritual anguish. Tortured, friendless, surrounded by enemies and apparently forgotten by God, he cried out again and again for help. He remembered past deliverances and looked for God's salvation once again. But the heavens were as brass. He heard no comforting voice and experienced no divine intervention on his behalf.

And we were all struck by the abrupt transition in the text. Weeping suddenly gave way to rejoicing. Dr. Weber raised the question: "What delivered the helpless sufferer? What so disoriented him from his misery that he could reach out to his people and the nations beyond in loving concern?" Obviously, his physical anguish remained. Men still rejected him, but somehow he was made free in his spirit. Apparently, in his powerlessness, he reached out in faith and grasped his God. "Though he slay me, yet will I trust him." And that made all the difference.

We were specifically challenged to think of Jesus Christ and his crucifixion. We were reminded that only he adumbrates the unidentified sufferer of this psalm. We reflected on his powerlessness in his "hour of darkness" when he took to his innocency all human guilt and shame, and received in himself, on our behalf, the righteous wrath of God against sin. All was powerlessness. And yet, in its mystery we recalled his triumphant cry of faith, "It is finished." Although crucified through weakness, he triumphantly embraced death. And his resurrection affirms the triumphant power of God.

The Prophets

We also examined Amos 5 and Isaiah 58. What searching words! What an indictment of all introverted pietism! How this message spoke to my heart! I had to accept the possibility that my most specific acts of worship and service in the name of Christ may be so wrongly based as to keep me from God's presence and separate me from his purpose touching God's mission in the world today. Shades of Matthew 7:22, 23! Not everyone who cries, "Lord, Lord," or who boasts of much service in his name will be accepted.

I cannot polarize worship from service. I cannot have one without the other. Both must be vocalized and demonstrated as acknowledgements that God is my Father and that I am caught up in Christ's purpose for the nations. I am called to be a pilgrim always moving outward from my worship of God in the closet and sanctuary to my worship of God in the service of the community. Only thereby can a man truly know salvation and "then . . . take delight in the Lord" (Isa. 58:14).

Salvation Tomorrow

It was a high moment when in plenary session we reviewed together the details of the sublime vision of God in the book of the Revelation (chapters 5-7). Glorious beings surrounded his lofty throne. They sang of his holiness and gloried in the truth that salvation belonged to him alone. The vast company of the redeemed gazed on the scene with grateful wonder.

Then the focus narrowed to a sealed scroll, the title deed to this world. But no creature was found worthy to take the scroll and establish God's authority over this soiled world. No one could be found to bring an end to all its evil. No one to rule in righteousness as King of kings and Lord of lords. No possibility of salvation tomorrow! John wept as we too have wept over the utter inability of human forces and churchly institutions to ameliorate even the rawest nerves of the human condition.

But one was found worthy. He was the Lion of the tribe of Judah. But this lion was revealed as a lamb slain, yet alive again. Again the mystery of powerlessness. But now the result of Christ's obedience unto death: all power in heaven and on earth had been given to him. He came forward. He took the scroll and began to break its seals. Swiftly the rapid sequence of judgment and deliverance commenced to unfold, to culminate in the final triumph of God in history. Salvation tomorrow? It is assured. God has spoken in his Word.

Salvation Yesterday

We read those familiar lines in Luke 4 that described Jesus in the synagogue in Nazareth, when he identified himself as the Servant of whom Isaiah prophesied. His messianic signs of deeds and words would confirm that the Kingdom of God was in their midst. And he looked for the response of faith of his townsmen. But he was rejected. His salvation did not come to the people and community that knew him best.

However, in other places he found those who would respond. He received them and they began to enter into his salvation. His own life style was to be their pattern. They were not to reduce his salvation to mere participation with the Sadducees and Herodians in playing the power game, although political action would become part of their total responsibility. He didn't encourage them to withdraw with the Essenes from the hard concerns of life and wait in the wilderness for the Last Day. Nor did he enroll them among the Zealots to advance his kingdom by fire and sword. And he warned them against the orthodox Pharisees who reduced the service of a loving God to an oppressive, compassionless legalism.

Jesus didn't identify "walking humbly with God" with an individualistic inwardness. His Kingdom represented the fullest integration of worship and service. The blind received their sight, the lame walked, lepers were cleansed, the deaf heard, the dead were raised, and the poor -- materially and spiritually -- had the good news of salvation preached to them (Luke 7:22). His kingdom was not in word only, but in power. As he preached he served and reconciled. Wherever he went he was as powerlessness to the unbelieving. But to those who believed, his power was graciously displayed.

Salvation Today

And yet, at this conference we have become impatient! Salvation yesterday? Yes! Salvation tomorrow? Yes! But what about salvation today? True, the Christ of history is the powerful Christ of tomorrow, but is there a living, powerful Christ today? My friends, we dare not forget Pentecost and the coming of the Holy Spirit into the church and upon the people of God. Great things have happened when in the past he was not a grieved and forgotten presence in the midst of the people of God. I trust we shall learn much more of him before this conference ends.

Actually, we've already been reminded of his presence and his power, bringing salvation today. Recall the sermon preached by the Rev. Wichean Watakeecharoen, the General Secretary of the Church of Christ in Thailand, at our communion service this past Sunday. He sought to remind us of the joy and victory of the Spirit by speaking of what he is doing in Thailand today, where less than one person in 1000 acknowledges Jesus Christ as Lord and Savior. Things are happening here. He told of "reports from many parts of the country bringing the news that youth and older people in large numbers are making the decision to accept Jesus Christ as their Savior."

In recent years I've traversed back and forth across this land in river boats, by bus, train and bicycle. I've been in Thailand's Malay mosques, Chinese temples, Buddhist halls and within the spirit fences circling its tribal villages. Out in the countryside I've stood before the great images of Buddha and pondered the spiritual condition of their devotees. No personal God on whom to call. No divine purpose, no meaning or movement to history. Nothing save the inexorable law of cause and effect; the iron law of retribution. And in the midst of this darkness the little Thai church has seemed so powerless.

But we were reminded that God is at work by his Spirit. His people are going out to their neighbors as never before in loving service. They respect their fellow-citizens, for all men bear the image and likeness of God. They participate with them in serving the community and in the common struggle for justice among men. This church is increasingly becoming the salt of the earth. But more, Thai Christians are speaking of Jesus Christ and proclaiming his gospel. Not the dialogue that drifts downward from religious discussion to community problems and then to the plight of man. Rather, the dialogue that moves upward and finally focuses on all that God has done through Christ to provide the elements which Buddhism lacks: linkage with the living God, the forgiveness of sins and eternal life.

Friends, much work is yet before us. Let us keep in mind an affirmation made by William Temple at an earlier international missionary convention. He said: "Our message is Jesus Christ. We dare not give less. We cannot give more."

This is salvation today.

10

The theology of salvation at Bangkok

This article by Peter Beyerhaus digs deeply under the surface and uncovers some theological implications of the "Salvation Today" conference that might not otherwise be noticed by reading the official documents. Predictably, Beyerhaus was a controversial figure at Bangkok. For example, his name was mentioned much more frequently in the daily conference newspaper than that of the new CWME Director, Emilio Castro, himself. Evangelicals will read and reread this incisive interpretation with much gratitude for such a clear evangelical expression.

PETER BEYERHAUS

When the theme for the eighth ecumenical World Mission Conference "Salvation Today" was announced shortly after the Uppsala Assembly in 1968, many evangelical minds all over the world rejoiced. With growing concern and anxiety they had watched how the Commission on World Mission and Evangelism (CWME) rapidly seemed to have lost sight of the preeminent goal of Christ's great commission, the eternal redemption of the unsaved "two billion" who by their sin, superstition and ignorance are separated from God, the fountain of life. Here the occasion for a clear reaffirmation of the biblical foundation, content and aim of Christian mission in view of the tremendous challenge of this crucial stage of world history seemed to be within the near range. Evangelicals knew, of course, that in view of the strong ideological cross-currents in the official ecumenical quarters theirs would not be an easy task. But still the issue at stake was too decisive not to give it a fair shake.

Thus very soon study groups were established, consultations were held and individual theologians got down to serious work. Nobody has seen yet a complete catalog of the documents which have been produced in this process and subsequently submitted to Dr. Thomas Wieser, the full-time study secretary

Peter Beyerhaus is Professor of Missions at the University of Tubingen, West Germany. He previously served as a missionary to South Africa. Beyerhaus is one of the chief architects of the Frankfurt Declaration, and his two most recent books in English are *Missions: Which Way?* (Zondervan) and *Shaken Foundations* (Zondervan).

for coordinating these efforts. Their number must, however, be considerable. This became evident also by the fact that the conference had to be postponed several times from the dates originally scheduled in 1969-70 to 1972-73. Although communication between the different groups was lacking deplorably, there is sufficient proof that despite vast contrasts in the theological quality of this material, some quite excellent papers have been produced. I am thinking particularly of the document of the Norwegian study group which was based on a masterly survey by the Oslo New Testament scholar, Prof. Dr. Edvin Larsson. The pity was, however, that these exegetical fruits were not made available to the public in time, nor was there any synopsis of agreements and disagreements which could have stimulated further research. Some very good Bible studies were distributed among the Bangkok delegates shortly before their departure; but they came too late in order really to be brought to bear on the deliberations of the conference. I actually observed in our chartered flight from Geneva to Bangkok, how the more conscientious participants made a last minute effort to go through these yellow papers which they had received just before their departure. The spokesman of the twelve-man Roman Catholic delegation, Fr. Hamer from Rome, in his fraternal farewell address to the conference on January 8, 1973, publicly deplored that better use had not been made of this most valuable theological study material.

It would, however, be wrong to assume that this failure in the theological preparation for Bangkok was due simply to organizational shortcomings. The six exegetical studies on the yellow paper, for example, had already been delivered at a biblical consultation in Bossey, March, 1972. But this event passed virtually unnoticed. The only fruit of this meeting which, as late as September, 1972, was made available to the constituency was a little brochure, "Biblical Perspectives on Salvation." This was originally designed as a more popular study guide to be used in congregations of the member churches. It was partly used in the Bible study groups in Bangkok, but found to be hopelessly inadequate, at least by the group in which I participated under the chairmanship of Greek Orthodox Bishop Anastasios Yanoulatos.

The real reason for the breakdown of the exegetical preparation for Bangkok was two-fold. First, it once more revealed the depth of the hermeneutical crisis in the WCC.

There is no common conviction that the Bible is the authoritative and reliable basis for Christian faith and ministry. Scripture is seen by many as a collection of different historical documents, testifying to the experiences of salvation and understandings of the divine will at the time they were written. But these witnesses, it is felt, do not necessarily agree among themselves, and they must be complemented by our own experiences in the different contexts of the human struggle today.

The second reason is that these present day experiences and quests now concern the ecumenical mind to such a high degree that they have become the starting point for seeking our solutions. Thus even the witness of the Bible (when it is consulted) is understood within the framework of current political, social, cultural, religious or psychological problems.

To this criticism, which was expressed in a study document from the Ecumenical Seminar in Tubingen, Dr. Wieser, in his "Report on the Study," replied in Bangkok: "The insistence on the uniqueness of the story in the Bible in the interest of affirming its authority, however, serves to accentuate the discontinuity between the biblical story and our historical situation today. Does this mean that the authority can only be affirmed, when it is one step 'removed' from our experience?" The evangelical answer to this question would, of course, be a clear "yes". The Bible can only exercise its role as the sovereign norm to evaluate our experiences if these experiences themselves are put to the test rather than becoming part of the norm themselves! Otherwise, contemporary man in his experiences and evaluations becomes the judge of the Word of God. Yea, he might even become the judge of God himself, as German "death-of-God-theologian" Dorothee Sölle, wrote in one of the preparatory papers: "That God does not weep in the Scriptures is bad enough for Him. He would have good reason to do so." Here, as we also find in several other texts prior to and during Bangkok, the borderline between theology and blasphemy has definitely been crossed.

Scripture, therefore, was not allowed to play its majestic role in Bangkok. It was complemented, or rather substituted, by a situationalist approach, called in the modern ecumenical jargon "contextuality." The real preparatory document for Bangkok, to which high importance was attributed by the organizers, from Secretary General Philip Potter downwards, was a

collection of documents called "Salvation Today and
Contemporary Experience." It culminated in an episode (taken
from the Japanese novel *Silence*), where in a given situation
apostasy from the Christian confession was held to be the most
relevant form of "Salvation Today." (This was reaffirmed by
Indian Jesuit Samual Rayan in the first issue of the conference
newspaper *Salvation Today*, December 31, 1972).

There was still another reason given by the Geneva staff as to
why the conference would deviate from the traditional
procedure of working on the basis of theological documents
prepared beforehand. This old method, it was said, would yield
too much to the Western way of theologizing. Westerners
reasoned on the basis of a scholastic system of dogmatic
categories in order to arrive at highly abstract formulas. This
would be both uncongenial to the minds of Christians in the
Third World and also irrelevant to their problems. Therefore, it
would be better to feed the conference material which would be
a more spontaneous expression of the Afro-Asian mind.
Personal testimonies, poems, songs, pieces of drama or liturgies
would be more appropriate. Even a dancing group was planned
through which some members could "explore the meaning of
salvation." Urged by the German delegation to produce some
solid theological documents for their personal preparation for
the conference, Dr. Gerhard Hoffmann, a newly appointed WCC
staff member, replied: "The group leaders are *not* tied to
definite texts. They can come with their own preparation but
they must face the insights of others who find other texts or
interpretations more important. For the other groups, too,
something analogous applies. Preparation is not possible on a
mere intellectual level, but rather by being tuned in to the
theme. This does not exclude an intellectual German theological
discussion, but it reduces the possibility to a 'contribution.' As
you state, the German delegation is crying for 'preparatory
material.' The first answer, therefore, would be: do not block
yourselves against an experiment in group dynamics, and still
less against the moving of God's Spirit, which is at least
possible. Rather prepare yourselves in a different way this time!
Is it not 'preparation,' if somebody somewhere discovers a new
song, contemplates on it and takes it along to Bangkok? Of
course he also may bring along biblical texts, which have just
become important for him."

This reply from Geneva served as an eye-opener to me as to

the real character of this conference. Although it was convened under a highly theological heading, serious theology was to be excluded from this conference from the very beginning. We rather were invited to expose ourselves to an experiment in group dynamics, which in America is more commonly known by the term "sensitivity training." Formerly, at the time of its crude origins in China, it was called "brain washing." That this was done in the name of the working of God's Spirit again bordered on blasphemy. Furthermore, the fact that it was done under the pretext that this was more congenial to the mind of the delegates from the Third World was rather an insult to their churches. Up to now Afro-Asian church leaders have given ample proof that they are quite capable of making their contribution to sound biblical theology. Or are ecumenical theologians like the late D. T. Niles already forgotten and disclaimed by the WCC in which they played such an important part?

In any case, Geneva had decided to stage this experiment in group dynamics, and the organizers were determined to carry it through. They seemed to be convinced that this would be the way to let the conference delegates arrive at their predetermined concept of "Salvation Today" without becoming aware that they were being manipulated by the shrewdest of psychological techniques.

The organizers of the Bangkok conference knew that if they would allow an open theological debate to develop, the results could prove highly unsatisfactory. Most likely a debacle quite similar to the polarization between ecumenicals and evangelicals at Uppsala, 1968, would have taken place. This would have meant that very few of these *recommendations* would have been passed. These recommendations were the central aim of the whole conference. They had been designed to build up the ecumenical action program in which the WCC "Program Unit on Faith and Witness" has been busily engaged ever since the time of the integration of the International Missionary Council into the WCC in 1961.

Therefore, from the theological point of view, Bangkok was a frustrating experience. After the first week of the conference, a leading American evangelical remarked to his friend, "This is the most boring meeting I have ever attended!" From the surface this seemed to be a general impression. The conference program, which was not disclosed before the beginning of the meeting, provided very few public lectures and still less opportunity to discuss the advertised theme. In fact, only the Geneva establishment itself was to be heard from the pulpit: Mr. M. M. Thomas, Chairman of the Central Committee, gave the one really theological address on "The Meaning of Salvation." He was followed by two reports, one by Dr. Potter as the previous director of CWME, and the other by Dr. Wieser on the proceedings of the "Salvation Today" studies.

The first week was composed of Bible studies under the general theme, "Exploring the Meaning of Salvation." The subsequent eight meetings of sub-sections and sections continued the conference work "with a view to action." Here lay the real emphasis of the schedule. Our objections would have been modified, if the Bible studies, i.e. the two Bible presentations of Hans-Roudi Weber in the plenary, as well as the three discussions in seven smaller Bible study groups had really been allowed to lay the theological foundations for the forthcoming ecumenical action program for mission. But Weber's Bible presentations were held as a panel performing a drama which culminated in catechizing the audience. This turned the whole thing into "a nice Sunday School lesson," as Bishop Chandu Ray remarked.

Some of the Bible study groups were perhaps the most pleasing part of the whole program. But when I inquired at the opening of our particular group meeting whether there was a chance to bring our results to bear on the findings of the whole conference, we were told again by those WCC representatives who were officially assigned to each group, that the groups were not supposed to produce any statements. The Bible studies were arranged mainly for our own spiritual benefit. In the context of the group dynamic experiment they seemed in fact to serve as preliminary stages in which, by the aid of our ecumenical sensitizers, we were gradually geared into the collective mind of the conference. Two of them did, indeed, produce quite evangelical statements, published on the bulletin board and in the conference paper. But only one became part of the final report of the assembly. Here it rather served as a biblical fig leaf to cover the humanist nakedness.

The main task for the working out of the final recommendations was, at least, nominally, assigned to the ten sub-sections, into which the three main sections were divided. But even they were not able to produce theologically-responsible statements. This was partly due to the deliberately disconcerted way of discussion, which could not lead to a real consensus of the group. In sub-section I-B on "Cultural Identity and Conversion," for example, even in the sixth meeting the participants were not able to agree whether there was something unique in Christian conversion as over against conversion in Maoism or in other religions. The report, therefore, had to be written by the chairman himself! This dilemma could be accounted for by the fact that the themes of the sub-sections were not introduced by biblically-oriented lectures or prepared drafts. Instead, "action reports" were given, to which the participants should respond by telling their own "experiences."

The "theology" of Bangkok, therefore, could be called the theology of experience. But even here not every experience was accepted as equally valuable. When a young evangelical from West Africa movingly related his conversion from Islam to Christ, this story was bypassed without any further comment or evaluation. Much, instead, was made of the story of a Chinese intellectual who in the cultural revolution was assigned to work in a pig stable, and thereby discovered his need to be "converted" to accept simple farm workers as his real fellow human beings. The theology, in this case, was that true conversion is not so much a religious experience as an overcoming of social estrangement.

By the way, Maoism was presented several times as a really acceptable alternative to Christianity. This became evident when on the China evening the stress was not laid upon the question as to how the gospel could be re-introduced to China, but on the contrary what the cultural revolution in China meant to our understanding of "Salvation Today."

This revealed, once again, not only the tremendous abyss between evangelical and ecumenical mission theology, but also the unwillingness of the controlling ecumenical organizers to allow a systematic analysis of this theological conflict and an open encounter. Some of us had foreseen this strategy at the beginning of the conference. Therefore, Dr. Arthur Glasser and myself seized the opportunity of the only public hearing after the three addresses of the WCC officials. We deplored that the one really crucial issue in connection with the conference theme, the ecumenical-conservative controversy on the theology of mission, which so clearly had been pinpointed by the

Frankfurt Declaration, had not even been mentioned in the director's report, "From Mexico 1963 to Bangkok 1973". We were both harshly met first by U Kyaw Than, the General Secretary of the East Asian Conference of Churches, and then by Philip Potter himself. Both employed their rhetoric to reduce the general conflict reflected in the Frankfurt Declaration to an internal quarrel among West German theologians. It should, therefore, not be allowed to embarrass the World Conference or, as U Kyaw Than mocked, to infect Asia by "theological tuberculosis." Having played on these racial sentiments, Potter succeeded in capturing sufficient emotional support from Third World participants to extinguish the threatening fire of a general theological debate in the plenary session. My proposal to the conference to call for an international theological consultation between ecumenical and non-conciliar evangelical theologians in order to resolve the "fundamental crisis in Christian missions" was never replied to. Nor was it taken to the vote, when I made it a formal motion on the last day of the conference.

Does this mean that Bangkok was really an atheological meeting? Several German participants stated that in Bangkok the Afro-Asian delegates, who formed the majority, had finally refused any further intrusion of Western theology into their churches. The call for a moratorium in sending Western missionaries to the Third World churches was interpreted accordingly. "Asia has finally been granted the right to be saved according to its own fashion," one radio commentator remarked. Especially African participants repeatedly stated their desire "to find their true identity" as the new slogan put it. This rather unbiblical concept seems mainly to imply a reformulation of Christianity within the framework of the cultural and religious heritage of the African past. The Kimbanguist Church, which claims to have received a special revelation and blessing of the Holy Spirit through the prophet Simon Kimbangu (In the minds of his followers he has been almost uplifted to the fellowship of the divine Trinity), was therefore highly acclaimed. It was represented as the outstanding example of such a genuine indigenous African church, which, without the cooperation of Western missionaries, had expanded rapidly and found its true identity.

I doubt, however, whether Bangkok really has meant the breakthrough of the Third World churches out of the former

Western dominance towards a theology which is both truly indigenous and authentically Christian. I also doubt that the loudest Afro-Asian speakers at the Bangkok meeting were really representing the faith of the masses of Afro-Asian church members. They have so often enjoyed the privileges of VIP's at ecumenical meetings around the world that they have lost the vital contact with their fellow Christians at the grass root level of the congregations. The influence of ecumenical sensitivity training with all its humanistic and syncretistic vocabularly has become tighter and tighter within their minds. Thus mentally and ideologically they have become even more dependent on the West than they were under the influence of so-called Western scholastic theology, which in most cases simply was plain biblical theology.

The deliberate appeal of the WCC officials to the African and Asian sentiments within the context of resurgent traditional religion in their post-Christian transformation has, of course, ushered in a dynamic give-and-take-movement. It might, finally, aim at the formation of an inter-religious, semi-political world church. Still all this is no spontaneous movement of the church in Africa, Asia and Latin America. The concept of "Salvation Today" which finally appeared in the official reports of the three sections, "Culture and Identity," "Salvation and Social Justice," and "Churches Renewed in Mission," was not the spontaneous, theological self-expression of those members appointed by their churches and mission bodies.

To arrive at a proper theological evaluation of the Bangkok conference it would be necessary to discern between two different conferences, which partly overlapped in Bangkok. The first and decisive conference had started long before the opening of the Bangkok meeting. It was the continuous consultation of the Geneva staff members and their accredited ecumenical fellow-workers in other parts of the world. This conference elaborated both the theology for "Salvation Today" and the strategy for Bangkok. The second, more representative, conference was the one in which the official delegates found themselves, carefully guided and guarded at every step by highly disciplined people who served as chairmen, secretaries, reflectors, consultants, artists, musicians, newspaper editors or rather anonymous sensitizers in the group meetings. The purpose of this official meeting, I'm afraid, was to arrive as nearly as possible at the predetermined results without giving

the impression that they had worked them out by themselves.
This master plan partly succeeded, but partly got stuck due
to the still intact biblical convictions of a great number of the
delegates from many different countries and ecclesiastical
traditions. This accounts for the rather uneven appearance of
the section reports. There are clearly evangelical affirmations
side by side with obtrusive expressions of current ecumenical
ideology. Compare, for example, the following definitions of
salvation and of mission in Section Report III-B:

Salvation is Jesus Christ's liberation of individuals from sin and all its
consequences. It is also a task which Jesus Christ accomplishes through
his church to free the world from all forms of oppression. This can only
happen if the church is renewed and grows. It is our *mission*
— to call men to God's salvation in Jesus Christ,
— to help them to grow in faith and in their knowledge of Christ in
whom God reveals and restores to us our true humanity, our identity as
men and women created in his image,
— to invite them to let themselves be constantly re-created in this
image, in an eschatological community which is committed to man's
struggle for liberation, unity, justice, peace, and the fulness of life.

One of the worst statements in the section reports is found in
"Litany" produced by Section I. It contains the following
strange combination of modern beatitudes:

You were a poor Mexican baptized by the Holy Spirit and the Blood
of the Lamb: I rejoice with you my brother.
You were an intellectual Chinese who broke through the barriers
between yourself and the dung-smelling peasant: I rejoice with you, my
sister.
You found all the traditional language meaningless and became an
atheist by the grace of God: I rejoice with you, my brother.
Out of the depths of your despair and bondage you cried and in your
cry was poignant hope: I rejoice with you, my sister.
You were oppressed and fled to the liberated areas and dedicated
your life to revolutionary struggle: I rejoice with you, my brother.
You were oppressed and put down by male authority and in spite of
sneers and snarls persevered in your quest for dignity: I rejoice with
you, my sister.

It would be completely futile to weigh the pros against the
cons and from such analysis proceed to a diagnosis of how near
the WCC at its Bangkok meeting has come to the biblical truth
and how much hope there might be for further dialogue,
cooperation and clarification between the ecumenical and the

evangelical movement. The "Program Unit on Faith and Witness" will by no means feel bound by any theological affirmations which do not clearly support its present strategy. It is far more important to notice which emphases have been put into the reports and recommendations either by continuous influence or last minute interferences by ecumenical activists. These really indicate the line of action which the WCC will follow during the forthcoming period of unchallenged executive power. "Now we are in business," one Geneva staff officer remarked, when those theologizing conference attendants had left Bangkok, who were not to be delegates to the succeeding assembly. The emphases on "Dialogue with Men of Living Faiths," on "Salvation Through Political Confrontation" and the "Moratorium" for Western missions are the decisive results of Bangkok, among which only the third is really new. One might term it an effort at the self-liquidation of the western missionary movement.

One last observation must be related. Before going to the conference we were informed that in contrast to the previous world mission conferences, Bangkok would not again produce theological statements which might be very orthodox in theology but which would not lead to action. Nevertheless, the section reports do contain theological statements in the form of preambles. These preambles were not the result of the discussions held in the sections. Before the conference itself was opened, accredited theologians had been asked to be responsible for their writing. In Section I they were Dr. Carl F. Hallengreutz of Sweden and Anglican Archbishop G. Appleton, of Jerusalem. In Section II the assignment fell on Professor Jurgen Moltmann from Tubingen. Only Section III was unable to produce a theological preamble. Since Dr. Nacpil from Manila was unable to attend the conference the statement of Rev. Koyama of Japan, whom the section chairman appointed in his place, failed to be accepted by the section. Therefore it was added as an appendix to the section report side by side with a theological statement which I had delivered in a panel discussion together with statements by Koyama and John Gatu from Nairobi. This sudden decision of Section III was one of the few really spontaneous events of the Bangkok conference.

As for the theological understanding of the theme, "Salvation Today," the preamble prepared by Moltmann is the most important one. It tries to bridge the gap between the evangelical concept of a predominantly personal and eschatological salvation and the ecumenical concept with its social, this-worldly emphasis by means of a "comprehensive notion of salvation." But Moltmann was challenged on three main points. First, he failed to acknowledge the basic distinction between the primary restoration of fallen man to the love of God with social reconciliation as its consequence. Second, his concept of anticipated eschatology makes man here and now the acting participant of that final salvation of the "groaning creation" (Rom. 8:19) which God has reserved for his own final redemptive act in the return of Jesus Christ. Third, Moltmann's yielding to the ecumenical idea of "contextuality" dissolves the concept of salvation into a number of widely disparate experiences. There is no clear recognition of the one basic reality of salvation which transcends all its specific expressions and consequences. Typical of this non-theological dissolution of the biblical message of Christ's universal salvation for all sinners who believe in him is the following statement: "In this sense it can be said, for example, that salvation is the peace of the people in Vietnam, independence in Angola, justice and reconciliation in Northern Ireland, and release from the captivity of power in the North Atlantic Community, (N.B. What would it mean in communist countries?) or personal conversion in the release of a submerged society into hope, or of new life styles amidst corporate self-interest and lovelessness."

Here under a seemingly biblical coverage, the concept of salvation has been so broadened and deprived of its Christian distinctiveness, that any liberating experience at all can be called "salvation." Accordingly, any participation in liberating efforts would be called "mission."

That this would be the Bangkok interpretation of salvation and mission was to be expected. The World Council of Churches should, however, not expect that evangelicals all over the world will accept it. We now are challenged to present the biblical alternatives by articulating our faith and by acting accordingly in obedience to Christ's Great Commission.

11

Dateline: Bangkok

HAROLD LINDSELL

The good ship *Oikoumene,* owned and operated by the World Council of Churches, slid off the ways at Amsterdam in 1948. It began its maiden voyage captained by Willem A. Visser 't Hooft, who set sail for the New Jerusalem. Now, twenty-five years and two captains later, the ship, loaded with close to three hundred churches, has run into stormy weather. Many people are asking where it is, where it is headed, and whether its compass is accurate.

A short while ago *Oikoumene* put into port at Bangkok, Thailand, for a World Conference on Salvation Today, sponsored by the WCC's Commission on World Mission and Evangelism (CWME). That conference, held from December 29, 1972, to January 9, 1973, was followed by the Third Assembly of the CWME January 9-12. The World Conference was attended by several hundred participants, the Third Assembly by 126 voting members.

The last major WCC meeting, the Assembly at Uppsala, Sweden, in 1968, had been attended by a substantial number of radical secularist theologians, and also by a large contingent of left-wing European and North American young people. The Bangkok participants were those interested in missionary matters, representing what to the evangelical observer is the best side of the World Council of Churches.

Two new officers took their places in the administrative structures of the WCC at Bangkok. Philip Potter, a West Indian who formerly was the director of the CWME, succeeded Eugene Carson Blake (who recently retired) as general secretary of the WCC, and Emilio Castro, a Uruguayan, took Potter's place as director of the CWME. And so two of the highest ranking officers of the WCC are from the third world.

To understand what went on at Bangkok, one needs some knowledge of the history of Christian missions for the past one hundred years. Noted historian Kenneth Scott Latourette called the nineteenth century the great century for missionary advance. The great advance began with William Carey in the 1790s. During the hundred years that followed, European and North American church-controlled and independent missionary agencies multiplied. For the most part the denominations and the independent agencies went their own ways without particular regard to other sending groups. With the dawning of the twentieth century a great change took place, a change that would at last produce the ecumenical movement and its structural form, the World Council of Churches.

The Ecumenical Missionary Conference convened in 1900 in New York, followed within ten years by the Edinburgh World Missionary Conference. At both, denominational and non-denominational missionary agencies were represented. The impulse generated by these missionary conclaves and particularly by Edinburgh led to the formation of two inter-denominational organizations: the Interdenominational Foreign Mission Association (IFMA), founded in 1917 and including in its fellowship the so-called faith missionary societies, and the International Missionary Council (IMC), formed in 1921, the constituent councils of which were open to denominational and non-denominational societies.

During the period between 1921 and the beginning of World War II, the IMC convened two international missionary conferences, one at Jerusalem in 1928 and the other at Madras in 1938. The papers from these conferences give evidence of wide theological cleavages. By 1921, theological liberals, schooled in German higher-critical rationalism, had captured many of the theological seminaries. A Pandora's box of variant and heretical theological views had been opened, and all sorts of deviations and accommodations crept out. Universalism, syncretism, theological inclusivism, as well as patent unbelief found adherents within the churches.

During this time several important events influenced missions. Karl Barth's work on Romans had appeared in 1918. In revolt against German liberalism, Barth sought a return to a revelatory and biblical theology, and he became the father and leading exponent of neo-orthodoxy. Later he wrote a massive systematic theology in which he dealt in part with God's election of men to salvation in Jesus Christ. Barth's idea of election opened the door wide to universalism, the view that all men are in Christ already, whether they know it or not, and shall at last be saved. Through this open door came the theology of Nels Ferré, Norman Pittenger, Bishop James Pike, and Paul Verghese, among others.

A second significant event was the publication of *Rethinking Missions* by William E. Hocking of Harvard as part of the massive *Layman's Foreign Missions Inquiry*. The United States had become the leading missionary sending nation in the world, and these books hit like a thunderbolt. The *Layman's Inquiry* vigorously assaulted the basic theological foundations on which missions rested. Latourette wrote: "Many of the most earnest of the constituency of the missionary enterprise cherished convictions which were quite the opposite of those represented by *Rethinking Missions*" (*A History of the Expansion of Christianity*, VII, 52). Virtually every American denomination had to justify and defend its foreign missionary program among its people.

Although at Madras in 1938 it could be seen that non-evangelical views had made progress in the missionary movement, the major decisions of that conference were evangelical in tone and the larger proportion of the career missionaries were evangelical in theology. The discussions at Madras centered on Hendrik

Kraemer's book *The Christian Message in a Non-Christian World,* which was essentially a response to Hocking's work. In a new preface to the second edition
Kraemer took pains to deny that his book was "fund-
amentalist," a charge circulated widely by critics of his
work. There was some uncertainty as to the meaning of
"biblical realism" as he used the term, but in the main
his thesis was quite clear. He laid the axe to the root
of syncretism, showing that any similarities between the
Christian and the non-Christian religions were actually
dissimilarities.

At the same time that the missionary agencies were
banding together, a movement was afoot to bind the
denominations together into a larger fellowship. In the
United States it took the form of the Federal Council of
the Churches of Christ, which later changed its name
to the National Council of the Churches of Christ in the
United States of America.

Meanwhile, on the international scene two other
ecumenical organizations appeared, their impetus having come in part from the 1910 Edinburgh missionary
conference. They were the World Conference on Faith
and Order and the Universal Christian Council for Life
and Work. These two organizations merged to form the
World Council of Churches at Amsterdam in 1948. The
WCC was similar to the National Council of Churches,
most of whose members joined the WCC, except that
it was international in scope.

The International Missionary Council, however, did
not join the WCC in 1948. It was still assumed that
missions was the business of the churches, and from
1948 on ecumenical leaders worked to bring the IMC
into the World Council of Churches. The problem was
that the IMC included in its membership non-denominational agencies and a number of evangelical mission
boards that wanted no part of the WCC, which from
its inception was theologically inclusive and had as its
announced intention the creation of one organically
united church. Finally, in 1961 the IMC was integrated
into the WCC as the Commission on World Mission and
Evangelism. It is interesting to note that the effort to

create unity was divisive in its outcome, for the faith missions, among others, quit the IMC when it went into the WCC.

The Commission on World Mission and Evangelism held an international gathering at Mexico City in 1963, and the recent one at Bangkok was its second. The Mexico City meetings showed that the conciliar movement was moving away from the historic conception of the mission of the Church. Whatever defects had attended the IMC conclaves at Jerusalem in 1928 and Madras in 1938, both of these conferences in their plenary sessions defined evangelism and the mission of the Church in rather traditional terms. By 1963, however, a substantial shift away from the historic position of the missionary agencies was evident.

In 1968 the WCC itself met at Uppsala, and the theological gaps that had appeared in the Mexico City CWME meetings became yawning chasms. The emphasis at Uppsala was on humanization, secularization, socio-political involvement, economic development of the third-world nations, the elimination of racism, revolution, and a virulent anti-American feeling that centered on the war in Viet Nam.

Uppsala clearly had a polarizing effect. Before the meeting took place, Donald McGavran of the School of World Mission at Fuller Seminary posed the question of what the World Council intended to do about two billion people who had never heard the Gospel of Jesus Christ. The WCC statement prepared before Uppsala was wholly unsatisfactory from an evangelical perspective. The Gospel of personal salvation through the substitutionary atonement of Christ on Calvary was supplanted by a secularized, this-worldly version of social action as the mission of the Church.

In an editorial entitled "Will Bangkok Be a Watershed or a Washout?," Paul S. Rees of World Vision, who has been as warm a friend of the ecumenical movement as any evangelical, picked out the observation by Visser 't Hooft (former general secretary of the WCC) that there is both a vertical and a horizontal aspect to the Christian faith, and that those who neglect the horizontal, i.e., "responsibility for the needy in any part of the world," are "just as much guilty of heresy as those who deny this or that article of the Faith." But at Uppsala the WCC, when considering the declaration on "Renewal in Mission," "fell between two stools," says Rees:

> It was not so much *thought* through as *tinkered* through, with the verticalists and the horizontalists making last-minute efforts to scotch one another by squeezing in a term here or a phrase there that would salvage *their* side of the debate. In the end neither side was satisfied. The horizontalists, alas, carried off more laurels than the verticalists.

Rees seemed to imply that the struggle is only a matter of over-emphasizing the vertical or the horizontal at the expense of the other. This interpretation is open to question. Rees does admit, however, that there are those who wish "to substitute humanization for evangelism," and quotes Dr. George Johnston, dean of religious studies at McGill University, who dismisses Christ's atonement on the cross and says "eternal bliss conveys almost no meaning."

The changes evangelicals at Uppsala secured in the "Renewal in Mission" report only served to highlight the basic differences, for they made the total report self-contradictory. It was evident that the WCC had departed from the positions it held at Amsterdam in 1948. The mission of the Church was now identified with social action, not with personal evangelism.

Against this backdrop the CWME met at Bangkok. In a report entitled *From Mexico City to Bangkok* the true nature of the struggle was delineated. The report stated:

> We see the debate revolving around three major problems:
> *1.* On the understanding of the Bible: Some see in the Bible the expression of unchanging truth which can be formulated and repeated. Others see salvation in the Bible as an ongoing event into which we enter.
> *2.* On the understanding of human history: Some see in the biblical story of liberation, in both Old and New Testament, direct scriptural support for the quest

for liberation, whether personal, political, economic or cultural. Others warn that the Bible is concerned with ultimate spiritual issues, not to be confused with temporal power struggles.

3. On the place of the Church in God's purpose and work for salvation: Many find it difficult to make a clear distinction, in terms of being saved or not saved, between the fellowship of the Church and human fellowship. Others insist that the boundaries of the Church as the *locus* of salvation must be maintained.

These statements about the Bible, human history, and the Church fairly represent the basic differences that exist within the WCC. To reconcile them is impossible except through a synthesis of opposites, and this, of course, evangelicals could not accept.

At Bangkok the divergent viewpoints surfaced quickly. On the first Sunday the Reverend Wichean Watakeecharoen, general secretary of the Church of Christ in Thailand, preached a thoroughly biblical sermon on salvation by grace through faith in Christ. The mimeographed conference journal that appeared the following day contained comments on that service. A German participant said Watakeecharoen's sermon was "very bad, representing the revivalistic theology of the Church of Thailand. The enumeration of 'so many souls saved' slaps the whole dialogue program in the face." No approving statements were printed, though some hearers were delighted with the sermon.

WCC staff member Thomas Wieser presented the first major paper to the conference, on the worldwide study of the theme "Salvation Today" during the four preceding years. The report noted the disparate opinions of what salvation is: from the concept of personal salvation from sin by faith in Christ, to the statement by the Methodist Church of the Ivory Coast that " 'salvation in the current sense means deliverance from illness, war, or slavery' and is associated by many with the deliverance from colonialism and forced labor." Wieser concluded his report by saying, "Reflectors will guide the conference in the task of interpreting the diversity of views and experiences in the light of Christian tradition."

If they did, it was not noticeable; no definitive statement appeared on what salvation really is.

The second major address was given by M. M. Thomas of India, chairman of the WCC Central Committee. He spoke of the need for spiritual salvation, saying that the mission of the Church "is to participate in the movements of human liberation in our time in such a way as to witness to Jesus Christ as the Source, the Judge and the Redeemer of the human spirituality and its orientation as it is at work in these movements, and therefore as the Saviour of Man today." Thomas went on to open the door wide to syncretism and to a denial of the uniqueness of Christianity:

> We are living at a time when we are deeply conscious of pluralism in the world—pluralism of human situations and needs, of varied religions and secular cultures, with different traditions of metaphysics, ideologies and world-views, in terms of which Christians themselves seek to express their commitment to and confession of Christ. So much so that any kind of a unity in the doctrine of Christ or of salvation in Christ, which has been the goal of traditional Christian churches, is to my mind impossible even of conception except in religious imperialistic terms. As a historian of religion, Wilfred Cantwell Smith, has recently said that on the grounds also of the loss of authority of the established churches today, "the old ideal of a unified or systematic Christian truth has gone. For this the ecumenical movement is too late," leaving a situation of "open variety, of optional alternatives," everyone choosing what suits him best (*Questions of Religious Truth*, pp. 34, 35). Then, of course, the question what kind of a criterion of Christian faith can we lay down in a pluralistic age, is sharply raised. Dr. Hans Küng, when he visited India recently, said that the criterion of faith could be that the believer should in some form acknowledge the Person of Jesus as "decisive for life," that is to say, to translate in my terms, decisive for the knowledge of Ultimate Reality and the realization of the ultimate meaning of life and its fulfillment here and hereafter.

His concluding remark was illuminating: "I leave all the unanswered questions for this conference of experts to tackle."

The third major paper was the report of Philip Potter, new general secretary of the WCC and formerly director of the CWME. Potter ranged far and wide and devoted more time to sociology, politics, and economics than to the Gospel and evangelism. This was not unexpected: the report was intended to give an account of "what has been happening in our world since 1963," and for this decade the controlling theme of the WCC and its agencies has been social action. Potter did admit that "there are strong voices which have claimed that the CWME has lost its integrity and its raison d'être through integration [i.e., by being incorporated into the WCC]. I hope this issue will be honestly faced at this meeting, for what is at stake is not merely a structural arrangement within the WCC, but our whole understanding of mission." Later he added, "Our fathers in the missionary movement avoided the pain of theological and ecclesiological controversy. We dare not." But when Peter Beyerhaus of Tübingen asked the conference to consider the theological crisis in missions as expounded in the Frankfurt Declaration, he was rudely and decisively rebuffed by Potter and by third-world spokesmen who argued that the Declaration was peculiarly German and was irrelevant to the third world. The Western world, the spokesmen said, should not export its problems to the third world. This effectively shut the door to any real theological controversy over the basic issues, even those already set forth in the *From Mexico City to Bangkok* booklet.

Potter, an articulate, friendly, and engaging speaker, used his position and power in other ways, too. It was he who told a reporter from the *Bangkok Post,*

> The eleventh commandment, "Thou shalt succeed," has led the world to the brink of annihilation. One doesn't have to look far to see how fear of losing has kept America's big power boys from accepting the fact that with all their massive efforts they have been beaten by the 'little yellow people' in Viet Nam."

Potter also pulled no punches when he said that "serious heresy" exists in the churches (i.e., WCC churches) on the part of those who profess the Christian faith but are not obedient to its demands to change the economic, political, and social structures. Since the minimal doctrinal commitment of the WCC does not deal with this matter and since churches are free to believe as they choose, it was hard to appreciate his "ex cathedra" judgment of what constitutes heresy. It was also Potter who, in his Christmas message to the churches, said that salvation equals liberation and that in Jesus's time salvation "signified liberation from all that impeded or restricted the life of persons and societies—whether sickness of body or mind, ignorance, indifference and fear, calamities of every kind, injustice by fellow citizens or by foreigners."

Apart from listening to the three major papers, participants in the conference and the assembly spent most of their time in section and group meetings. Out of them came a plethora of pronouncements but no clear, unambiguous statement of the meaning of salvation today, yesterday, or tomorrow. The public bulletin boards did reveal some interesting opinions on the matter. One sign proclaimed that "People matter; people suffer; salvation is in sharing suffering." Following an unscheduled session on China in which one delegate praised Chairman Mao as the saviour, this sign appeared: "Salvation=God save China from 'conversion.'" Professor Moltmann of Tübingen diagrammed his view of "salvation in, by and through economic justice, political freedom and cultural change." Some participants thought that the theological statement of Section II, largely the work of Moltmann, should stand as the "theology of Bangkok," but WCC staff member van den Heuvel reminded the conference that theological perspectives had also come from conference addresses, worship experiences, conversations, drama, and art.

The spirit that brooded over participants was one of powerlessness, frustration, and despair. This was true not only of the evangelicals in the WCC, some of whom openly expressed sorrow over the lack of emphasis on evangelism and the fulfillment of the Great Commission, but also of those whose interest lies in a gospel

of social salvation. Perhaps it was best expressed by
the prayer that came from Section I:

> For Christ's Church on earth,
> confused about its message, uncertain about its role,
> divided in many ways, polarized between different
>   understandings,
> unimaginative in its proclamation, undisciplined in
>   its fellowship,
> we pray: Out of the depths we cry unto Thee, O
>   Lord!
> For ourselves in this Conference,
> overwhelmed by our impressions, torn apart by
>   prejudice,
> often in doubt, plagued by frustrations,
> struggling for honesty, for understanding of each
>   other,
> crying for love, searching for justice,
> we pray: Out of the depths we cry unto Thee, O
>   Lord!

Right now the WCC is in a crisis situation, for it
appears to be unsure of its message, its mission, and its
mandate. The good ship *Oikoumene* has been afloat
for a quarter of a century; now it remains to be seen
whether the new helmsmen, Potter and Castro, can keep
it off the shoals.

Among the things the World Conference and/or the
CWME Assembly did were:

1. Blasted the United States and President Nixon on
Viet Nam in a statement generously larded with such
phrases as "ruthlessly destroyed," "blasphemous mockery of peace making," "holocaust of destruction,"
"brutal power politics," "sinister example of imperialism," "wanton destruction," and "blind reign of terror."
"In this war salvation is at stake," the statement said,
although "the Christian community itself is divided on
this issue." (84 ayes, 11 nays, 20 abstentions.)

2. Condemned Portuguese colonialism in Southern
Africa, particularly Angola, with a recommendation
favoring Christian support of the national liberation
movement. In the assembly an amendment to include
racism in Uganda as also wrong was defeated by a vote
of 20 for and 30 against.

3. Approved an affirmation from Bible Study Group 3 that stated in part:

To the individual [Christ] comes with power to liberate him from every evil and sin, from every power in heaven [!] and earth, and from every threat of life and death. To the world he comes as Lord of the universe, with deep compassion for the poor and the hungry, to liberate the powerless and the oppressed.

4. Approved the report of Section II, which said in part:

a. Our concentration upon the social, economic and political implications of the Gospel does not in any way deny the personal and eternal dimensions of salvation. Rather, we would emphasize that the personal, social, individual and corporate aspects of salvation are so inter-related that they are inseparable.

b. There is no economic justice without political freedom, no political freedom without economic justice. There is no social justice without solidarity, no solidarity without social justice. There is no justice, no human dignity, no solidarity without hope, no hope without justice, dignity and solidarity.

c. Salvation is the peace of the people in Viet Nam, independence in Angola, justice and reconciliation in Northern Ireland and release from the captivity of power in the North Atlantic community . . . [but not in the Warsaw Pact!].

5. Approved the report of Section I, which said, among other things: "Our eyes will be keenly open to discover what *He* is doing among people of other faiths and ideologies." "Other living faiths . . . have a mission." "We shall rejoice in the common ground we discover."

6. Urged "missionary agencies to give serious consideration to the resolutions by the WCC Central Committee in Utrecht concerning the withdrawal of investments from Southern Africa."

7. Recommended that serious attention be given to the possibility of supporting and encouraging local groups of action and protest against unjust economic structures (e.g., groups organizing a boycott of U. S. imports in areas of U. S. economic domination).

8. Expressed "particular concern regarding relationships between conservative evangelical groups and churches traditionally related to conciliar groupings."

9. Voted that the CWME would "offer its services and make itself available to the Congress of World Evangelization to be convened at Lausanne, July 1974."

10. Agreed "to promote and support self-tax of individuals and churches everywhere as an expression of transfer of power from the powerful to the powerless" (a resolution initiated by the X minus Y Action, an action group in Holland).

Conspicuously missing from the meeting: any condemnation of Communist oppression and exploitation; any reference to subjugated peoples such as the Czechs, Hungarians, Poles, Latvians, Lithuanians; any reference to the Communist Warsaw Pact, though the North Atlantic Treaty Organization was panned; any criticism of socialism, despite repeated criticisms of capitalism; any adequate recognition of what God is doing through the Jesus movement, Key 73, the Berlin and other congresses on evangelism, Campus Crusade for Christ, or mass evangelism; any emphasis on the two billion unreached people without Christ or any genuine enthusiasm to harness the resources of the churches to finish the task of world evangelization according to the terms of the Great Commission (which I never heard mentioned during the entire gathering).

The WCC seems obsessed with the vision of establishing a truly just society among all men, saved and unsaved, atheistic Communists as well as committed Christians. Beneath the surface there lurks the terrible danger of the false promise of a golden age among men, an age of a world without injustice or oppression. Such a vision represents a sad misreading of history and reveals a mistaken view of the nature of man. The WCC is to be commended for its concern for social justice, and every Christian in and out of the ecumenical movement should likewise be concerned. But attempts to do away with injustice and oppression should be based upon one cold fact: oppression and injustice can be alleviated, in some areas considerably reduced, but they cannot be eliminated, even as the individual Christian can be improved in his personal life but not perfected so long as he is in the flesh. Sin will be with us until Christ returns, and as long as sin persists there will be injustice and oppression of all kinds. The problem will remain insoluble, though partially remediable, until sin is eliminated forever; no human efforts, no earnest pronouncements, and no illusory idealism can alter this basic fact.

Virtually nothing was said at Bangkok about the command of Christ to evangelize the world, i.e., to finish the task of preaching the Gospel of personal repentance and faith to all men. Nor was anything said of the two billion who have never heard the Gospel, except in a single sentence in which Philip Potter dismissed the debate over this matter as futile. There was no clear-cut sense of the lostness of men without Christ and the fact that if they die in their sins they are eternally separated from God. The great stress on salvation as liberation from political, social, and economic oppression might very well have been just as much at home in a purely humanistic or secular conference.

Bible Study Group II seemed to get a little closer to the truth in its statement that "salvation can only be conceived as liberation from sin." But the statement goes on to say: "It is necessary, however, to state clearly what sin means and to name without fear its present forms, especially its social and political forms." Nowhere was sin or liberation from it clearly defined in the biblical sense. Sin is the lack of conformity to the will of God. While sin may be manifested in corporate ways, responsibility always lies at the doors of individuals. Society as such cannot commit adultery, for instance; individual sinners do this. Salvation in the biblical sense means the removal of the guilt and penalty of sin for those who come to God through Jesus Christ. It also means the beginning of deliverance from the power of sin in the individual's life and the end of the presence of sin when Christ returns.

From all this, then, some conclusions:

1. The CWME and the WCC have in them a substantial number of people who are theologically evangelical as well as a broad spectrum of other views from a pale liberalism to extreme ideological leftism.

2. Control of the ecumenical movement lies in the hands of those who are not theologically evangelical. Evangelicals exist by sufferance; their presence is welcomed, but they have no place in the power structure.

3. Neither Uppsala nor Bangkok produced any full-orbed statement about salvation, conversion, evangelism, or the mission of the Church that is biblically sound and therefore acceptable to evangelicals. Indeed, their statements are inimical to the evangelical viewpoint. The breach has been widened very considerably since Amsterdam in 1948.

4. Evangelicals within the WCC have been looking for encouragement and help in the pursuit of what they believe to be the major mission of the Church (the taking of the Gospel of Christ to all men everywhere, in the power of the Holy Spirit and with the hope that soon their king, the Lord Jesus, will return). Their expectations have been disappointed.

5. Evangelicals within the ecumenical movement have much more in common with their evangelical brethren outside the ecumenical movement than with non-evangelicals in the WCC. But many non-conciliar evangelicals have refused to join hands with their brethren who through church affiliations they cherish are related to the WCC. This has made impossible an alliance of all evangelicals in the cause of missionary outreach.

6. It is time for evangelicals in and out of the WCC to join together to do what all of them are committed to do as believers in the Great Commission of the Lord Jesus, i.e., to finish the task of world evangelization as soon as possible. The International Congress on World Evangelization, which will convene in Lausanne, Switzerland, in 1974, should give the most serious consideration to the creation of some form of continuing fellowship or organization that will have for its binding power a common commitment to the task of world evangelization.

7. Evangelicals should say to those who truly believe that salvation is deliverance from political, economic, and social oppression: "You do your thing and we'll pray for you; we'll do our thing and you pray for us."

8. Evangelical unity and commitment to the evangelistic task are not enough. There must be a vital spiritual renewal in which the Holy Spirit provides the dynamic required to complete the Great Commission as well as persevering and prevailing prayer, without which no spiritual movement can get off the ground.

Will evangelicals catch the vision, see the possibilities, join hands, and move out for Christ in this new way? □

12

THINKING ALOUD ABOUT BANGKOK

Paul L. Rees

It is reported that Benjamin Franklin, emerging from the stormy concluding session of the Constitutional Convention in which the form of government of the United States had been hammered out, was accosted by a lady who asked, "What kind of government do we have?" The weary Franklin snapped, "A republic, madam, if you can keep it!"

In 1948 the World Council of Churches was formally constituted as an association of denominational groups having in common the purpose to "confess the Lord Jesus Christ as God and Savior according to the Scriptures and therefore seek to fulfill together their common calling to the glory of the one God, Father, Son, and Holy Spirit." (The phrase "according to the Scriptures" was added to the original sentence at the Third Assembly of the Council in 1961.)

By 1972 the number of church bodies that had affiliated with the Council stood at 252, their aggregate membership running to approximately four hundred million in 90 countries. Thus the World Council of Churches has become an historical entity that is nominally more embracive of the non-Roman Catholic Christian world than any agency the churches have ever known. The WCC is not a creedal body. Its minimal trinitarian and Christological confession is intended to bind the participant churches together as being unashamedly Christian. However, each affiliating church continues to regard its own creed as the confessional standard by which it orders its life and witness theologically. If it is remiss in this ordering, the fault cannot justly be laid at the door of the Council.

On the other hand, the Council, notably through its Commission on Faith and Order, has demonstrated that, far from being a front-runner for theological indifferentism, it is willing to tackle the most sensitive and controversial theological issues, to face them straightforwardly, and to encourage thoroughgoing debate with respect to them. The purpose of these discussions and the reports thereof is not to commit the Council as such to particular doctrinal positions but to clear the air for a better understanding by each affiliate of the theological position taken and confessed by other affiliates. For a long time the suspicion has been growing in knowledgeable circles that basic doctrinal commitments are not so intransigently opposed to one another as to necessitate the incredible organizational dividedness of twentieth century Protestantism. The World Council of Churches, in my judgment, is *not* in difficulties today because of these aims and concerns, which ought to be shared by all serious-minded students of the Holy Scriptures and of the Church's mission.

As for the charge, sometimes made, that the WCC is a lobby of rabid advocates of a world super-church, one has simply to say in all honesty that no official document has been passed by a World Council Assembly making any such commitment. That here or there one might find a WCC bureaucrat who would like to have it so, I do not doubt. But that is another matter. The fair-minded investigator is honor-bound to weigh the solid evidence.

Meanwhile, since 1948, the church bodies that comprise the WCC have been exposed to the heavy weather created by the theological radicalism that has enchanted the novelty-seekers, exasperated the classicists, and enraptured the journalists. The God-is-dead phenomenon was the most journalistically marketable of the numerous spin-offs of a theological mood that denigrated or defied both Scripture and tradition.

The demise of God-is-dead radicalism came fairly quickly. More enduring have been the attempts to give theological respectability to universalism, syncretism, humanism, demythologism, existentialism, and something we may call violentism.

Coupled with theological considerations, are sociological, political, and cultural developments of the past quarter-century that have altered the whole balance of relationships between the Occident and the Orient, between the whites of the world and the coloreds, between the free world, the communist world and the "Third World" of the uncommitted, between the haves and the have-nots, the developed and the developing, the nations with atomic warheads and the nations without them.

When, therefore, I think of the World Council of Churches, whether in a plenary gathering such as Uppsala in 1968 or a divisional meeting such as the recent Bangkok gathering of the Commission on World Mission and Evangelism, I think of a broad forum where Christian men and women from a hundred backgrounds, traditions, cultures, prejudices, and concerns come together to witness and to learn, to get angry and to show love, to reflect their biases and to defend their convictions (sometimes without knowing the difference between the two), to protest and to proclaim. And, through it all, the good and the bad, the wise and the foolish, to believe that the Lord of the Church Universal is still walking in the midst of His golden candlesticks, speaking grace and judgment!

As an ordained minister in a communion that is not affiliated with the World Council of Churches—the Evangelical Covenant Church of America—I have been invited to attend, and have attended, the Evanston, New Delhi, and Uppsala Assemblies of the WCC. I have been asked to address, and on one occasion did address, the Commission on Faith and Order. Although I was not present at Bangkok, I have read the record and the documents so far available, as well as a number of reports that have appeared in the religious press.

I am not surprised at the variety, even the absurdity, if you will, of some of the theological input at Bangkok. It is almost inevitable, given the fantastic doctrinal pluralism that has overtaken the denominations in recent years. I am, at the same time, grateful for signs that Bangkok was at least a step in advance of Uppsala. In the Uppsala section on mission the trend was reductionist on the side of Christian roots (the essentiality of Christ, the Cross, and conversion) and expansionist on the side of Christian fruits (the reshaping of social structures and the humanizing of life). Bangkok, it seems to me, was more aware of the indispensable complementarity of these two concerns.

Bangkok appears to have been marked by a more serious grappling with what the Bible has to say to us on the theme of salvation than perhaps any previous meeting of the CWME, perhaps indeed than most comparable conferences held by non-Council Christians.

At the same time one is bound to say that Bangkok and the reactions to it provide further proof that conciliar and non-conciliar conversations alike are vexed by inadequate terminology. The more negatively critical we are toward the WCC the more we tend to polarize our judgments around the two words "ecumenical" and "evangelical." It is a thoroughly confusing and unscholarly way of mangling words. If men such as Leslie Newbigin and John V. Taylor and James Scherer and John Gatu and Douglas Webster and Pierce Beaver and Eugene Smith and John Coventry Smith, are impliedly non-evangelical because they are actively ecumenical, then words have ceased to be decent carriers of important meanings.

It should be possible for evangelicals, whether conciliar or non-conciliar, to speak lucidly about views that can never be reconciled with evangelical faith as known and witnessed to from New Testament times to the present. In the January 1972 issue of the *International Review of Mission*. which was devoted to pronouncements preparatory to Bangkok, a contributor wrote:

> Deliverance from sin brings up the problematic of God; eternal bliss conveys almost no meaning. Atonement by Jesus on our behalf is just as implausible since He is so distant in history and so unlike most of us. . . . "Behold the lamb of God, who takes away the sin of the world". . . . But the Lamb of God idea is certainly no more at home in the modern world than the claim that Christ wrought atonement for us by dying on a cross.

This is evangelicalism repudiated, and needs to be faced as such. Is "atonement by Jesus on our behalf" any more "implausible" to city dwellers in modern London or Tokyo than it was to dwellers in ancient Corinth, to whom, according to St. Paul, "the preaching of the cross is foolishness?" For nearly twenty centuries the Good News the world *needs* to hear has been that of the implausible, and indeed impossible, acts of God in Christ—Christ crucified, Christ risen, Christ forgiving, Christ re-creating—"for us men and our salvation." This is the givenness of the gospel whose dimensions and implications, to be sure, need to be skillfully illustrated and persuasively acted upon in keeping with the mood and mentality of our times, but whose central core must never be supplanted or eroded.

Evangelicalism, which need not be identified with sectarianism, fundamentalism, legalism, or Westernism, is concerned with that aspect of reconciliation between God and man, and man and man, that would still be necessary if wealth were equally distributed the world over and social justice reasonably held sway everywhere.

Full well do I know that some evangelicals have contributed to the imbalance between personal pietism and social activism, and that therefore we should be tolerant of those witnesses who overstate the case for social restructuring. Nevertheless, it would be vastly helpful to the cause of an authentic Christian solidarity in evangelism and mission if both parties to this particular dialogue would display less dependence on the ambiguities of jargon and greater insistence on the value of clarity. Say what we will about words, the crafting of our terms and sentences is important.

One is tempted to feel that the most objective and persuasive critiques of WCC affairs in general and of the CWME in particular are those that are being produced by concerned persons who operate within the framework of the WCC.

I cite Dr. James A. Scherer, professor of World Mission in the Lutheran School of Theology at Chicago, as one example of what I have in view. Professor Scherer faulted the materials that were produced in preparation for Bangkok at three points, each of them related to the theme of the conference: "Salvation Today." Let me comment on the inadequacies that he listed.

1. "Failure to Deal with Mission as an Act of Faith." Scherer rightly feels that we deal too shallowly with the theme of "Salvation Today," if we think of salvation as a concept that, from the point of view of modern man, is obsolete, or ambiguous, or remote. This obsolescence, or ambiguity, or remoteness, is held to be the creature of twentieth century developments of reform and liberation. This, to Professor Scherer, is a misreading of the situation. "The underlying problem," says he, "is that contemporary movements add little or nothing to the once-for-all given basis and foundation of the Christian mission in God's reconciling act in Jesus Christ. The motive and power for mission are not found in the questions and cries of the world—though from such questions and cries we can get valuable guidance for the direction and carrying out of our mission."

In this connection it needs to be said that Bangkok provided a celebrant occasion for this emphasis on the *givenness* of the gospel, and the summons to believe in the gospel's crucified and risen Lord, to emerge. It came out in the form of an Asian testimony. Consider the following passage from the conference Communion sermon, which was delivered by the Rev. Wichean Watakeecharoen, the general secretary of the Church of Christ in Thailand:

> During this past year 1972, reports from many parts of the country bring the news that youth and older people in large numbers are making the decision to accept Jesus Christ as their Savior. . . . The aim of the Church of Christ in Thailand is to double its membership during the four-year period, 1970-1974. . . .
>
> At the present time in Thailand there are many young preachers whom God is using in the work of evangelism. Their preaching is a clear witness to Jesus Christ. As they preach, they invite all who have never received Jesus Christ as their Savior to stand up and acknowledge Him publicly. . . . The Holy Spirit is at work in His Church.

That such a happy report given on a eucharistic occasion was not intended to mirror either the sole methodology or the total burden of evangelism should be taken for granted. Allowing for the much more that might have been said, let me affirm that to many of us that picture of the living, witnessing, growing church is consonant with the official mandate that was given to the Commission on World Mission and Evangelism when it was established as the successor of the International Missionary Council in 1963: "to further the proclamation to the whole world of the gospel of Jesus Christ to the end that all men may believe in Him and be saved."

What has to be faced is the fact that to a considerable number of conferees at Bangkok the language of the Thai Council secretary and the language of the published aim of the CWME are alike archaic and unacceptable. Why? Several factors contribute to the explanation, but one of them is the loss of conviction that Buddhists, for example, do in fact need to be converted and that faith in Christ is the central issue in the converting process.

2. The second weakness that Professor Scherer deplored in the Bangkok preparatory materials was, as he captioned it, "The Tendency to Fragment the Comprehensive Character of Evangelism." His use of the word "comprehensive" is explained in the sentence, "Though it is divine in its origin and source, salvation manifests iteself comprehensively as an event with social and political, as well psychic and personal, dimensions."

But now comes the crunch. Dr. Scherer felt—and so published—that the "preliminary documents seemed to imply that the complementarity of witness and service, of proclamation and presence, formerly upheld in ecumenical statements on evangelism, is now very likely a thing of the past." He feels that just as many traditional evangelicals have failed to take seriously the summons to social responsibility and action, so now a preponderant number of ecumenical minds are prepared to mute the Christological issue in the Church's mission and settle for social amelioration and liberation.

"The Assembly," he wrote, "should resist every tendency to dissociate salvation as proclamation from salvation as service and involvement at points of human need."

It strikes me, on reading the reports and proposals that have come out of Bangkok, that this tendency was, on the whole, only mildly resisted. I find it disappointing that Philip Potter, director (until last year) of the CWME, in his report to the Bangkok conference, should quote without modification or exception a statement on "dialogue" produced by a "consultation on this vital subject in 1970:"

True dialogue is a progressive and cumulative process, in which communities shed their fear and distrust of each other, enter into a living together in dialogue. It is thus a dynamic contact of life with life, *transforming each other and growing together.* (Italics added).

This, Dr. Potter insists, is not "a betrayal of mission" but rather a "new tool for mission."

The Apostle Paul at times engaged in dialogue but he would have been horrified by this definition of what he was doing. The last thing he wanted was to have his gospel *transformed* by the input of the Pharisees, or the Stoics, or the Epicureans. He didn't want the word of the cross *transformed.* He wanted it *believed.* What Dr. Potter approvingly quotes comes dangerously close to being an obscuration of the gospel, not an explication of it. It is the novely of such language that makes responsible evangelicals, whether WCC oriented or otherwise, wonder if what is being achieved is a theological phantasmagoria unrecognizable by any criteria that arise out of the New Testament.

Dr. Potter now carries the immense responsibilities of the general secretary of the World Council of Churches. He has many things going for him. He has a quick and brilliant mind. He has a "Third World" background, which is an asset on the international scene today. He needs the love and prayers of Christians around the world. It was all the more unfortunate, therefore, that at Bangkok he so unqualifiedly endorsed the 1970 Consultation's definition of dialogue with men of other faiths.

Also regrettable, one may say in passing, was the following categorical pronouncement:

The fact of one world has held out great prospects for the world mission of the Church. The eschatological words of Christ have become very vivid and urgent: "This gospel of the kingdom will be preached throughout the whole world (oikumene), as a testimony to the nations" (Matt. 24:14). This has created a lively debate in missionary circles as to whether the emphasis should be on proclaiming the gospel to the two billion or more who have never heard it in the lands which have lived for millenia by other faiths, or whether it should be preached literally to the whole world, including the so-called Christian lands of Europe, North America, and Australasia. This debate is totally futile when we look closer at this one world in which we are living.

The debate may have been characterized by exaggerations, distortions, or omissions, but it would have been far wiser if the general secretary had not dismissed it so cavalierly as being "totally futile."

· *3.* The third weakness that Professor Scherer spotted in the pre-Bangkok documents he calls the "Danger of the Loss of the Transcendent and Universal Dimensions." He feels that liberation and humanization movements, however timely, can be perilously illusory without the informing mind and the transforming love of Christ. Of such movements he writes:

> Seeking freedom from a state of human powerlessness, they exhaust themselves in the development of man as a unit of production and consumption, sacrificing the transcendent dimension which includes part of the "truly human." In both cases there is the tendency for the immediate and the particular to become the ultimate; the eschatological promise of universal fellowship with God within the Kingdom is frustrated and negated."

He adds:

> The Christian mission to the world will also become barren and sterile if it negates or minimizes its Christological substance. Salvation, properly understood, includes both liberation and humanization; but it includes more. Only as men are brought into dialogue with the living Christ and under the influence of His gracious healing and enlightening presence will liberation and humanization follow. We must heed the warning issued by the apostles to the religious establishment of their day not to sacrifice or suppress the very treasure of our faith, and the very heart and center of our assurance: Christ *for* us (as Lord and Savior), Christ *in* us (as the Holy Spirit, and equipment for discipleship), and Christ for the *world* (as mission and apostolate). For if we do not confront men with the whole Christ, the manifest Christ, we too are judged for falsifying or suppressing the testimony to the gospel.

There were notes sounded at Bangkok that expressed this concern and confessed this faith. A statement drawn up by Bible study number 3 called an "Affirmation on Salvation Today" was adopted by the conference as its "Celebration Statement." After exalting Christ crucified and risen as the "sovereign Lord of all" it enunciates both the personal and social concerns of the gospel and the responsibility of the Church for participation with Christ in His "saving activity."

It is to be hoped that the churches, in receiving this message, will be as "action oriented" on the personal front of evangelism as they will be on the corporate front, as concerned with a *man* who needs saving as with a *social institution.*

Concludingly, let me make three observations against the backdrop of Bangkok.

1. The first has chiefly in mind the variegated community of non-conciliar evangelicals. It is not enough for us to exhaust our energies in an exercise of castigation against the WCC because it has made the "social gospel" its stock in trade. Our cliches are threadbare. Our thinking is greatly in need of a freeing up that is both biblically and historically defensible. In eighteenth century England John Wesley told the Methodists that God had raised them up "to spread Scriptural holiness and reform the nation." Result? Britain got thousands of newly converted men and women pouring into the life and fellowship of the churches but, beyond that, it got some evangelically motivated legislation that drastically altered the face of British life.

Traditional evangelicals today are too ready to be critical onlookers as the struggles for a better society go forward; or, if not that, are ready to back only those "safe" reforms that will protect elected behavioral taboos. For the most part, we lack prophetic robustness and legislative conscience with respect to the deeper issues of race, poverty, war, economic exploitation, substandard education for minorities, and the like. The call of WCC groups for Christian social thinking that is action-oriented has some vigorous and suffering seriousness behind it. Much better and more discerning treatment than to be dubbed "pink" or "Communist." Its excesses here or there should not blind us to its best insights.

2. My second observation is that both conciliar and nonconciliar evangelicals might well take some of their critical heat off the WCC and its agencies, and put it, with brotherly candor, on the communions that make up the WCC. It is in our denominational seminaries that much of the theological radicalism is spawned and much of the downgrading of evangelism takes place.

Few things in all of church history have been sadder than the faddism and flatulence found on seminary premises in the past thirty years. It is here—notoriously in the United States—that what Robert Fitch, himself a seminary dean, once called "egghead religiosity" coins its jargonistic phrases and reels off its curious novelties: "religionless Christianity," "churchless religion," "the God beyond God," "demythologized Scripture," "mature secularity," and dozens of others.

It is in this climate of theological confusion that school and church come fastidiously to disdain, in Fitch's words, "vulgar evangelism," "contamination by a cross."

This is no plea for seminaries that are choked by tradition. It is a plea for seminaries that are concerned both with roots and revolutions. They could help the cause of a healthy ecumenism.

3. My final observation relates to Christology and mission. The ultimate question which the Christian mission addresses to all men is, What will you do with Jesus Christ? Is Jesus the man at the same time the incarnation, in datable time and visible form, of the eternal Son of God? All else in the Christian affirmations springs from this—the unsullied life, the reconciling death, the authenticating resurrection, the living, loving, redeeming presence to whom the Holy Spirit bears witness through the Scriptures and the Church. This is the core of the Christian confession. This is the launching pad of the Christian mission. To withdraw from this is to abdicate the mission.

It happens that exactly forty years ago Professor Edwin Lewis of Drew Seminary, Madison, New Jersey, shook the foundations with an article in

Religion in Life which he called "The Fatal Apostasy of the Modern Church." The article was expanded into a book entitled *A Christian Manifesto*. The *Manifesto* was notable for several reasons, not least of which was its personal confession of return form a good-and-great-man view of Jesus to the God-man view, on which the first Christians built their creeds and launched their mission in the world.

In an earlier book Professor Lewis had paid Jesus the compliment of being "a man who achieved perfect divine sonship." Then, one day, he was challenged by the thought that this was not the faith of the early Christians. The faith they confessed was that Jesus was "God manifest in the flesh." It was this faith, as Lewis was obliged to acknowledge, that made the Christian Church, the faith in fact without which we would not have had the Church.

Now let me give you Professor Lewis:

You have the right to refuse your assent to such a claim: God 'respects the integrity of human personality,' even to the extent of allowing it to decide against Him, to resist what would seem to be His most irresistible appeal, and to nullify the result of His most divine deed. But you have no right to claim that you can refuse to believe that God was personally incarnate in and as Jesus Christ and at the same time be a witness to the world of the faith that originally gave birth to Christianity.

Or again:

More more important than the words we use is what we use the words to *mean*. I am willing to listen to any man's statement of his understanding of Christianity. I am willing that he abandon, if he so desire, all the traditional "thought-forms" and "patterns," as we perhaps too glibly say, and invent, or at least employ, a totally new vocabulary. But when he has done this, I shall still want to know what his *meaning* is. Does the new statement express in a more vivid and compelling way the ancient truth that "God was in Christ reconciling the world unto himself?" Or is it new not only as respects the *form* but also as respects the fundamental *thought?* In the end, that must be the question which every alleged "reinterpretation of Christianity" will have to meet; and I make bold to say that it will be to most "reinterpretations" a rock of offense upon which they will come to grief.

It is this kind of historical and theological realism that needs to inform the thinking of many ecumenical leaders at the moment. A watch's hairspring is of little worth if the mainspring is broken. Define evangelism any way we may. It is not, in essence, what the early Christians meant by it if we discard what Professor Lewis called the Gospel Figure (Jesus Christ), the Atoning Deed (the Cross), and the Impregnable Rock (the resurrection.)

Ten years ago Bishop Stephen Neill, an ecumenical pioneer, observed that "conversion" was becoming the missing word in WCC literature. (Shortly thereafter it made a reappearance in some useful but not very potent studies). This year, 1973, Professor Scherer, a friend of the WCC, writing in a Lutheran theological journal, declares that "Evangelism is in danger of becoming a forgotten word in ecumenical circles."

Are these comments by Neill and Scherer fantasies? Or are they portents?

Recalling the Ben Franklin episode with which we began the question may be asked, What have you in the WCC? Answer: a council of churches—*if you can keep it!*

What have you in the CWME? Answer: an agency mandated to "further the proclamation to the whole world of the gospel of Jesus Christ to end that all men may believe in Him and be saved"—if you can keep it!

Epilogue

Arthur F. Glasser

*In the debate, the mission confided
by Christ to all his disciples was
not considered; the world with its
expectations and needs was overlooked;
the biblical message was not invoked;
the intentions, devotion and love of
the missionaries, with their mistakes
and methods, were not taken note of..."*
(SEDOS 73/159, reported in Mission
Intercom of the U.S. Catholic Mission
Council).

Bangkok was a frustrating experience for Evangelicals.
You have read their reactions in this book. It confirmed
their pessimism regarding the Ecumenical Movement. Even
those who had been optimistic and hopeful that Bangkok
would eventuate in a new understanding between Evangelicals and Ecumenists found the outcome rather sobering.

This does not mean that Evangelicals came to Bangkok
determined to be suspicious and negative. The pre-
conference literature spoke of opening up the debate on
SALVATION TODAY "as widely as possible". Presuppositions
would be exposed and discussed in order "to reduce the
element of arbitrariness and subjectivity". The Bible
would be heard. Its witness to salvation and the missionary task would be thoroughly reviewed, even celebrated!
And Evangelicals would be welcomed!

147

Some Evangelicals were hopeful that Bangkok would re-
verse the position on Mission taken by the World Council
of Churches at its Fourth Assembly in Uppsala in 1968.
At that time, the WCC had so minimized the Mission of the
Church as biblically defined and traditionally performed
that Evangelical protest was loud and continuous. Evangelicals prayed and encouraged one another to believe that
Bangkok would be different. Would not its delegates be
more mission-oriented than the leaders of the WCC? And
were not its Reflectors told that in their day-to-day control of the agenda, they should deliberately aim for "balance in the presentation of the main theme"?

Were some Evangelicals unduly naive because they sought
to take the pre-Bangkok literature at face value? Did
they really believe that the delegates would seriously
grapple with such realities as the lostness of all men
apart from Jesus Christ, the centrality of the task of
Gospel proclamation, the tragedy that at this late hour
in the history of the Church two billion have yet to hear
of "salvation today", the cruciality of gathering converts
into growing and multiplying congregations, the participation of all Christians in the freedom, fellowship and
service of Christ, and the need to generate in the hearts
of God's people a new zeal for His glory among the nations?"
If some Evangelicals were hopeful of a new direction being
taken at Bangkok by the Ecumenical Movement, it was only
because of their growing awareness that within the WCC
there were not a few men of "like precious faith".

As Bangkok progressed, however, Evangelicals found themselves caught up in its tension, struggle and restlessness.
Basic questions surfaced that demanded far more attention
than the conference could possibly provide. For instance,
under whose Authority and by what normative Rule is the
mission of the Church to be performed? If Holy Scripture
is the rule of faith and practice, how shall it be regarded?
A collection of unrelated diversity or God's revelation of
His ongoing redemptive purpose that climaxed in the death,
burial and resurrection of Christ? Is the canon of this
Revelation closed or open? Dare its Authority be super-
seded by contemporary voices whether Christian or non-
Christian calling for a drastic reconception of the missionary task? Among other things, would this not negate
any essential difference between Christians and non-

Christians? And this could mean that "Salvation Today" is either achieved by works or received by grace? All which brings one to the place where he is uncertain as to whether God is a philosophical concept or a Personal Being, who is both transcendent and immanent. And where does His Spirit enter the picture? Does He do His main work in the world through the Church according to the precise framework defined by Christ or does He work independent of it? (John 16:8-15)

Throughout the conference, first one and then another expressed the hope that Bangkok's divergencies would come to a focus in Jesus Christ. He is the Head of the Church, the Saviour of the World and the only true God. Evangelicals warmed to M.M. Thomas' ringing affirmation that "Jesus Christ, crucified and resurrected, is the only God worthy of man's worship and obedience." But they later wondered whether this Indian scholar felt Buddhists and Hindus and Muslims and Jews should be converted to Him. And would Bangkok affirm that He is Lord, and that His Great Commission is the Church's great priority, to be obeyed with all the heart, will, conscience and resources at its command?

This is not the place to judge whether or not Bangkok accomplished its objectives. One must read the official documents and decide for himself. In this epilogue my objective is merely to relate what took place for five successive days in an upper room where some 20 delegates were assigned to explore the theme: "Growing Churches and Renewal". How we happened to be chosen for this assignment was not directly explained. All we knew was that our official designation was Section III, Sub-section B, and that we had a keen Evangelical, the Rev. Seth Nomenyo of Togo as our leader.

From the outset it was apparent to the members of this study group that none of their members was convinced in the least that Philip Potter was justified in flatly contending that it was "totally futile" to focus attention on the two billion who have yet to hear the Gospel. "Isn't that what a conference on World Mission and Evangelism is all about?" argued our Chairman. And we agreed. We largely reflected the old IMC concern formulated by John R. Mott that "the Gospel can and should be brought within the reach of every creature within this generation". As a result, we

brushed aside the suggestion of the East Asia Christian
Council that we "deal with new relationships between
churches around the world". In this day of wide recepti-
vity to the message of Jesus Christ, Christian mission
should not be confined to a preoccupation with the inter-
relatedness of churches already in existence.

We began by listening to one another speak of the ways
in which God is liberating men in our day through the Gospel.

Rev. Chul-Ha Han drew our attention to Korea. He spoke
of his joy in starting three churches. "It is my habit
when I have no church to serve on Sundays". We asked,
"But what are your reasons for doing this?" He replied,
"I have three reasons: 1) I was overwhelmed with fear that
should my people die without hearing the Good News, I would
be held responsible; 2) I also have been possessed by the
vision of people everywhere leading a peaceful life around
the Church; 3) And God's Word has come to me as it did to
Paul at Corinth (Acts 18:10): I have much people in this
city." Good reasons!

Then Rev. Ardi Soejatno took over and described the growth
of the Church in Indonesia in the face of Muslim, Hindu and
pagan opposition. He spoke of the Gospel as "the power of
God for salvation" (Romans 1:16) and of the "word of the
cross" as God's wisdom (I Cor. 1:18,24). He expounded these
texts in the context of Java today. He spoke of the manner
in which the Gospel makes men new creatures in Christ, en-
hances the position of women in society, stimulates education, and furthers the national consciousness of the people.
We queried him as to the unprecedented post-war multiplica-
tion of congregations among people who formerly were Muslims.
In no time at all he was at the black board, chalk in hand,
drawing mysterious diagrams and enthusiastically speaking of
the mission of the people of God in Indonesia today. Their
efforts to express their unity in Christ, their vigorous
witness to the Gospel, their careful nurturing of younger
Christians, and their self-less service on behalf of non-
Christians have produced an irresistible "people movement"
among Indonesia's millions. We were fascinated. Shades of
the old International Missionary Council with its deliberate
aim of proclaiming the Gospel "to the whole world to the end
that all men might believe in Him and be saved"!

By this time Tess Sition could contain herself no
longer. An attractive Indonesian youth leader, she felt
the time had come to speak her peace about Bangkok. Although barely twenty, she evidenced both spiritual growth
and moral courage. With engaging charm she proceeded to
take the Church apart: "Can't the leaders see? We young
people want plain words. We are sinners. Christ came
and died for us. He is the One who heals us and delivers
us from the evil powers. He reveals His will in the Bible.
We young people who follow Him know what's wrong with the
Churches. They are filled with people who haven't been
born again! Yes, that's it! They aren't yet Christians.
We young people want Bible studies in which we might hear
these things. Isn't it the mission of the Church to teach
us the Bible and help us get saved?"

What could one say? Here was a prophetic voice speaking
plainly of "Salvation Today". We responded with smiles of
encouragement and an amen or two. As Rev. Nomenyo had said,
"That's what Bangkok is all about!"

Others contributed. Bishop Chandu Ray described the growth
of the Church in Singapore. Canada's Archbishop Dean shared his
delight in a biblical approach to the missionary task. Daniel
Ratefy spoke of the way in which the enemy of souls had over-
reached himself in recent events in Madagascar with the result that the Church there was growing as never before.
Furthermore, through its young people it was actively participating in the reconstruction of the nation. Other
representatives from the Third World expressed their conviction that God was mightily at work in the world today,
drawing men and women to Himself through the Gospel.

In the end we agreed that the key was the Bible. But the
Bible must not be regarded as a collection of rules for
right conduct so much as a means of grace for man's salvation. When men ponder its message, the Holy Spirit does his
work of awakening and converting. Archbishop Dean was ada-
ment about this: "It seems that church growth flourishes
best in situations closely related to the study of the
Scriptures. Where that kind of devotion goes on the seed
grows quietly, secretly and suddenly appears." This explains the growth of the Church in Taiwan and Korea, and it
shall be the key to the coming growth of the Church throughout the Near East. This latter opinion was confidently

affirmed by Rev. Albert Isteero, of Egypt and Lebanon.

Finally, our attention was focussed on the Communist
world, particularly Eastern Europe, through the moving
contribution of Frau Hildegard Fuhl of East Germany. She
spoke of shrinking churches of a hostile atheistic State,
of restrictions against teaching Christian truth to the
young, of the declining role of the clergy.   "We can't
speak of renewal through church growth. Our churches are
declining in membership. We can only pray that God will
renew us despite this. Then too, it seems as though He is
pressing us to look at ourselves in the mirror of Marxism.
We've come to see our Church's past failures, especially
its failure to serve in social matters. And, we were not
God's prophetic voice in the land when it was possible to
be a prophetic voice. Now, we must ask ourselves what our
mission is to be. Our country has become a missionary
situation. 'Jesus' is becoming an unknown word for most
of our younger people. You say that when men read the
Bible, God speaks. But biblical criticism has diminished
the willingness of our people to listen to the Bible. What
are we to do?"

We listened in silence, burdened for our brethren throughout the Communist world. Then our dear brother Ratefy
spoke. Behind his words was the long experience of a per-
secuted, suffering Church in Madagascar. He spoke gently,
but firmly: "You want your people in East Germany to turn
to the Lord Jesus Christ. You want Him to enlighten every
home with His Presence and His Rule. Why is this so?
Because of what Jesus Christ has come to mean in your own
heart and life. Now, don't forget the treasure which God
has committed to you. You were saved by the Gospel. Your
vision is that this Gospel will be known and believed throughout Germany. But don't forget that a vision will fade and
die out unless it is shared. Start multiplying small Bible
study groups. Start one in every home that opens to you.
Share the Gospel with each separate group. And believe God.
In time you will bring life to individuals, to their families, to communities, to the whole nation. This was the
way it happened in our country. They took our Bibles from
us. We still met together, and quoted to one another the
Bible portions we had previously memorized. They tried in
various ways to silence us, but to no avail. And do you
know what happened? Lives were touched. We increased in

numbers. We grew and grew and grew. Today, throughout
our country our people are hearing the Word of the Lord."

Dr. Beyerhaus also contributed to this discussion. He
spoke of the movement of history, of the coming of the
Last Day, and of the appearance of Antichrist. He reminded us that God had decreed that all human history
would be consummated in Jesus Christ. Would the churches
be growing in that dark and final hour before Christ's
glorious appearing? Who could say? In some places the
people of God might find their backs to the wall, facing
total catastrophe. They would not likely be growing in
numbers. Their experience might not be unlike the situation in certain totalitarian countries today. And yet
they could always count on God's faithfulness. By His
Spirit, he would make possible the renewal of their in-
ward man, right up to the last moment.

On this note our discussions ended. Before we parted,
however, we drafted a brief statement of what we felt
had to be the heart of any gathering convened to consider "world mission and evangelism". Some excerpts follow:

1. Each generation must evangelize its own generation.
   The concerns of *church growth and renewal* are the
   chief, abiding and irreplacable tasks of Christian
   mission.

2. The outworking of one's individual salvation cannot
   compare in difficulty and complexity with the outworking of God's salvation in and through the visible
   community.

3. The Church may grow in members and in doctrinal understanding, but may lack an awareness of the call of
   Christ to participate with Him in liberating society.

4. The Church may deepen its spiritual quality and
   social service, but may lack an awareness of the
   call of Christ to participate with Him in beseeching
   those who do not know Him to be reconciled to God.

In conclusion, we would like to state what has seemed
to us to be the central fact of all our reflections...Our
mission is to call men to Jesus Christ...to implore them
to accept God's salvation, and to help them grow in faith
and in the understanding of Christ...

DATE DUE